International Salon of Contemporary Art

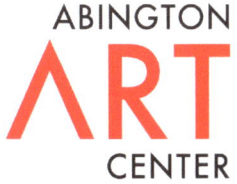 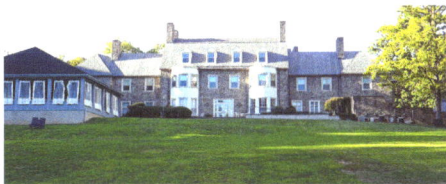

Exhibitions
Friday, April 6, 5:00 p.m. - 8:00 p.m.
Saturday, April 7, 11:00 a.m. - 5:00 p.m.
Sunday, April 8, 11:00 a.m. - 3:00 p.m.

AvantGarde M&A is holding its annual Exhibition of the contemporary artists. We warmly invite you to visit the Exhibition and attend the Awards Ceremony at the Abington Art Center 515 Meetinghouse Rd, Jenkintown, PA 19046 Artists will be present to discuss their works.
The opening reception will take place Friday, April 6 from 5 p.m. to 8 p.m

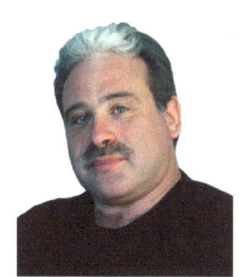

Lev A. Kushner
AvantGarde
M&A

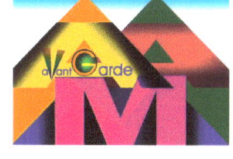

Cover
Kora Velikhanly,
New York, USA

2018

Please visit
www.GardeAvant.org

INTERNATIONAL SALON OF CONTEMPORARY ART

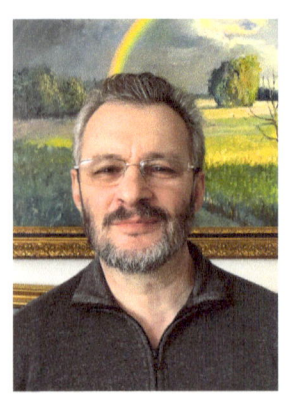

Gennadiy Kaplan

Gennadiy Kaplan was born on November, 26, 1957 in the City of Korosten' in Ukraine. His career as an artist began in 1980 after he finished high school and graduated from Kubansky (Krasnodarskiy) State University with a Master Of Art and Technical Graphics.

The very first exhibition of Gennady's paintings took place in the art department of the University in the year of 1979. His still life and landscapes were highly graded by both, the professors and the students.

Since 1980 he has taught in the Central School of Art in the city of Sochi, Russia. The beauty of city and surrounding nature inspired him to paint numerous beautiful paintings. Between the years of 1982 and 1999 the artist lived and worked in Kiev, Ukraine. His paintings were displayed in mobile exhibitions, including Andriivs'kiy Descent. During that time Gennadiy 's paintings were also presented in Museum of Ivana Kavaleridze.

In 1999, Gennadiy Kaplan and his family immigrated to the United States, and 2 years later, in January 2001 nine of his paintings were exhibited in the JCC Klein Branch in Philadelphia. After that the artist's paintings were presented in the Art Gallery of Itshakov, center city of Philadelphia (2003-2004), Turo Gallery,Bryn Athyn,PA (2004-2006), Riverbank Arts Gallery, Stockton, NJ (2006-2008), Congregation Beth Or, Maple Glen, PA (January 2008), Old City Jewish Art Center, center city of Philadelphia (2009), Won Buddhist Philadelphia Temple, Glenside, PA (2010-2013). Today the artist still likes to work with many different techniques, such as oil, water color, pastel, its. Paintings of Gennagiy Kaplan represent him in many different countries and most of them may be found in private collections.

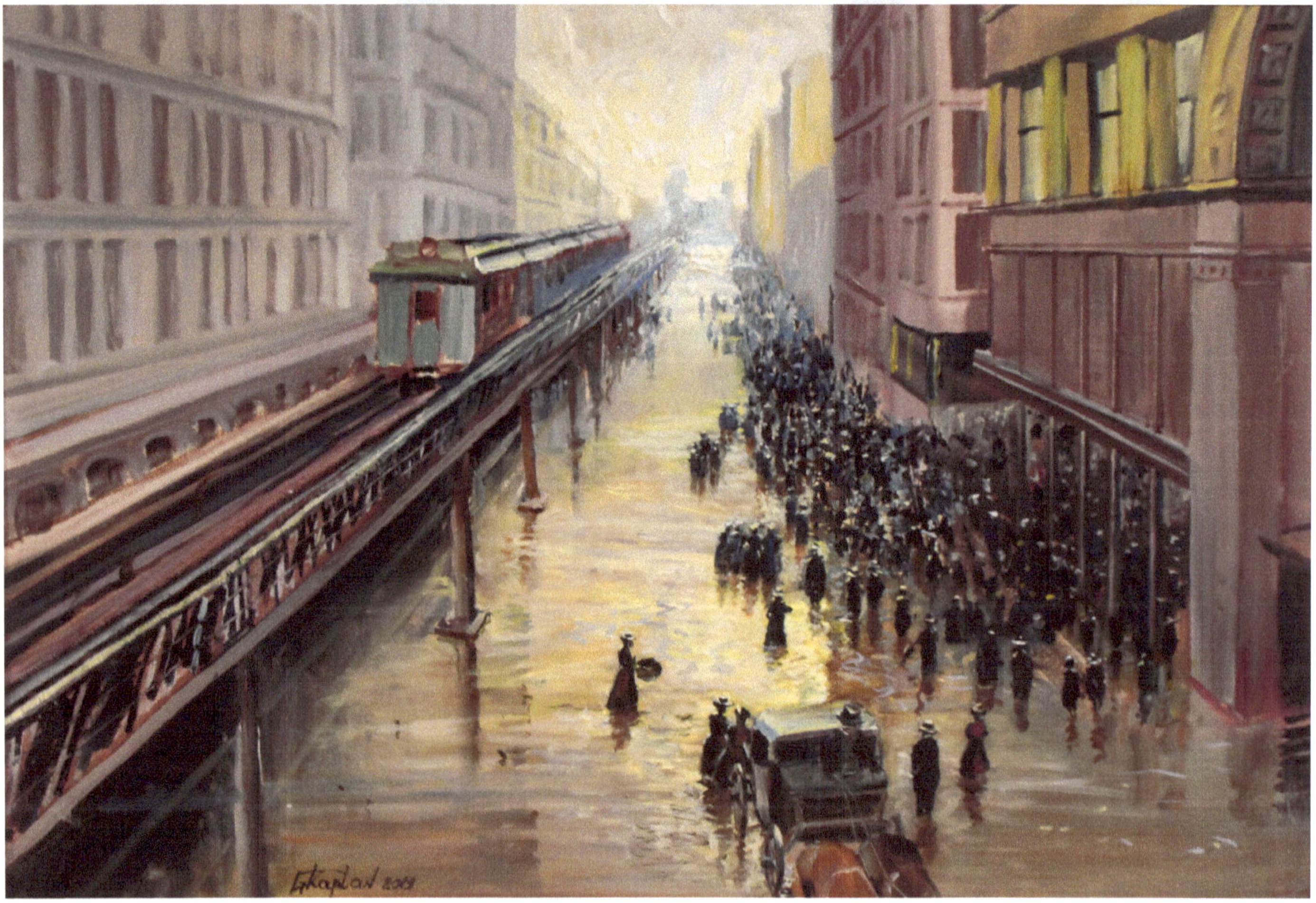

Old New York, can/oil, 2013, 23"# 36

WWW.GARDEAVANT.ORG

APRIL 6 - 8, 2018

International Salon of Contemporary Art

Gennadiy Kaplan

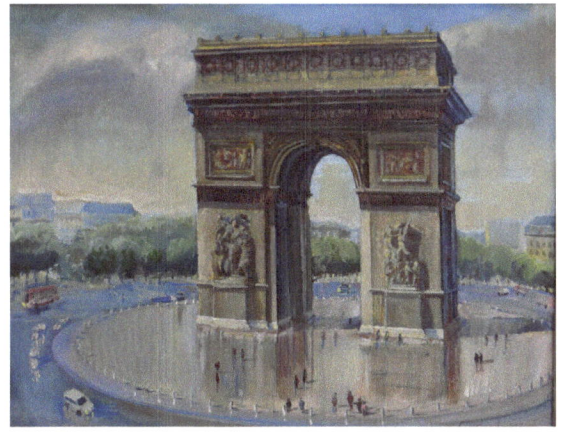
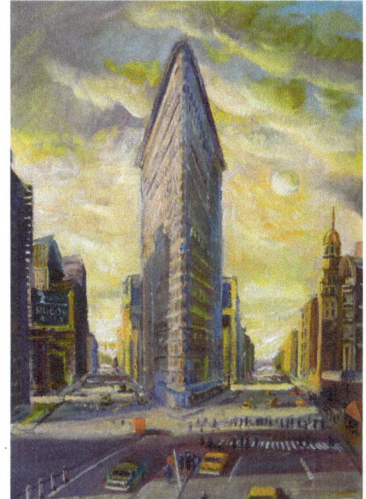
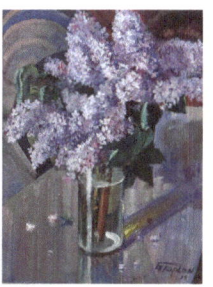
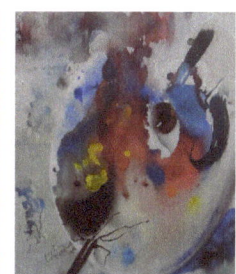
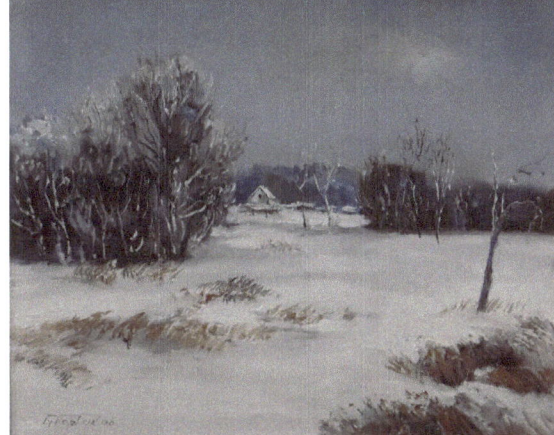
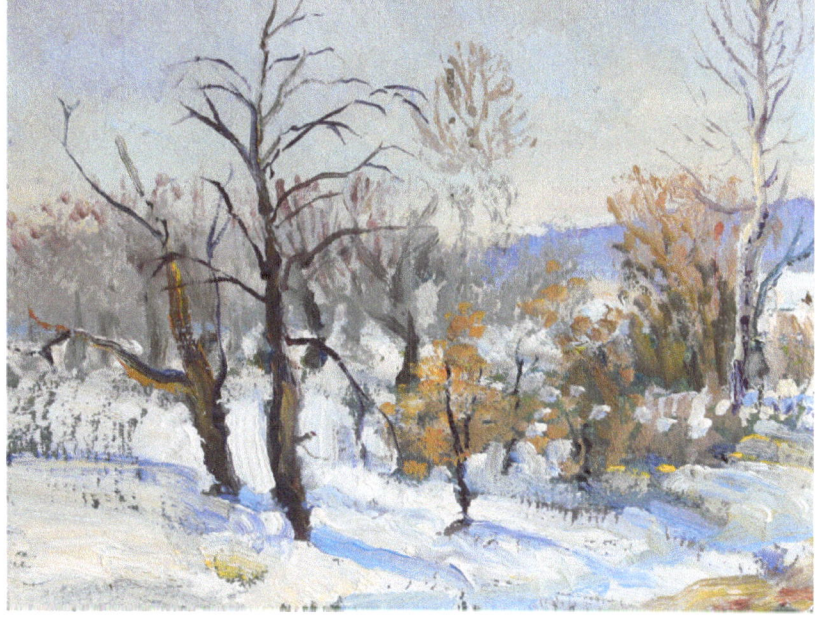
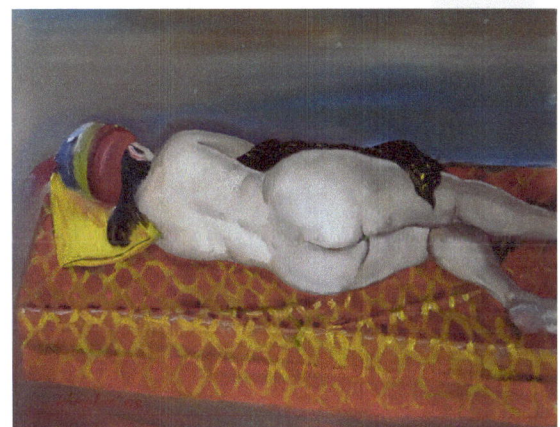
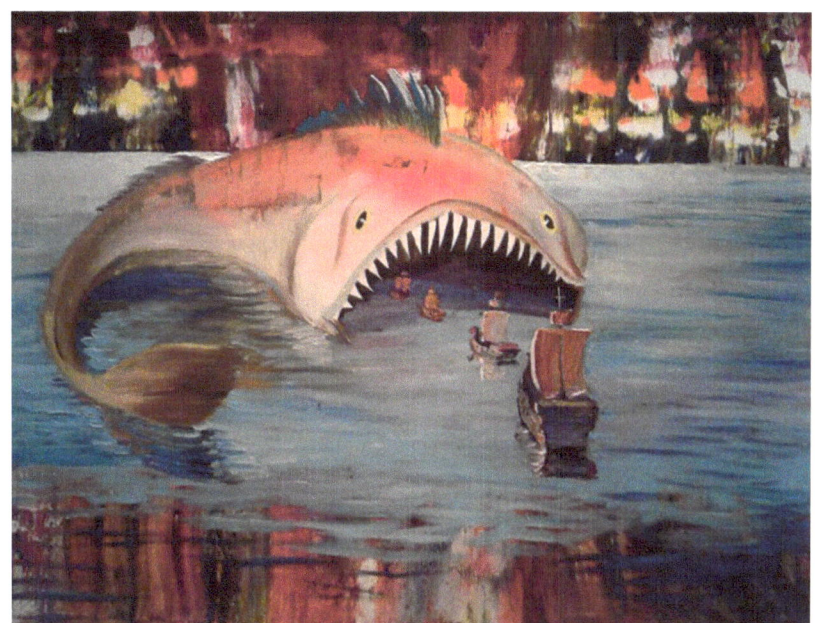
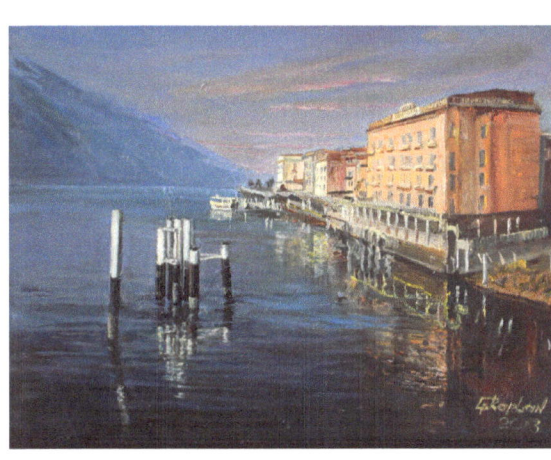

WWW.GARDEAVANT.ORG   APRIL 6 - 8, 2018

INTERNATIONAL SALON OF CONTEMPORARY ART

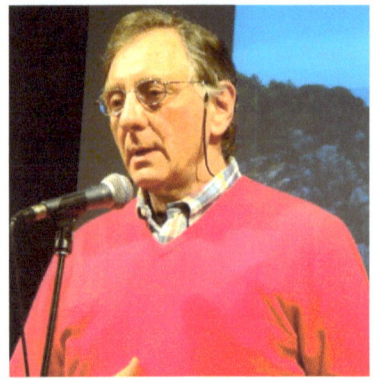

Vitaly Rakhman

Vitaly Rakhman was born in Crimea on the site of the ancient city of Khersones in 1945. At age 6, he started taking special classes for sculpture and drawing and continued his education at the Moscow Strogonov's Art and Design Institute. He received several state awards for industrial design. In 1974, Rakhman took part in the famous nonconformist artists Izmailovo Exhibit for which he was exiled to Siberia. In 1980, he immigrated to the United States and in the Philadelphia, Pennsylvania area since 1982, where he attended the University of the Arts. In 1997, he founded the publishing company, Vital Connections, Inc. His newspapers currently serve the Russian community in the Northeast United States. A author of two books of poetry, Rakhman also participated in several group and solo art shows.

We live in a scrappy world of the Reality and Illusion, the speeding world of changing images and points of view, in the world of cliches and mass production.

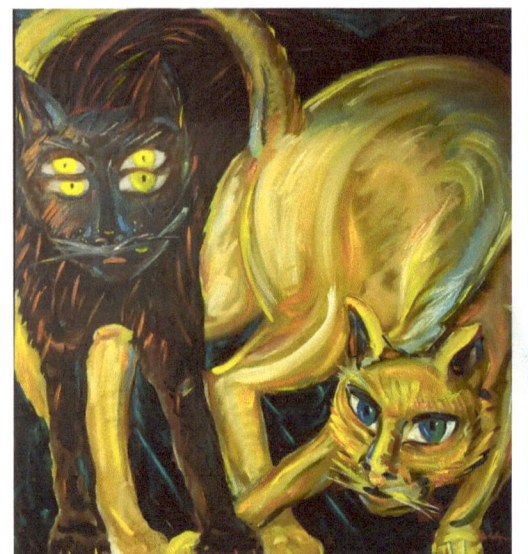
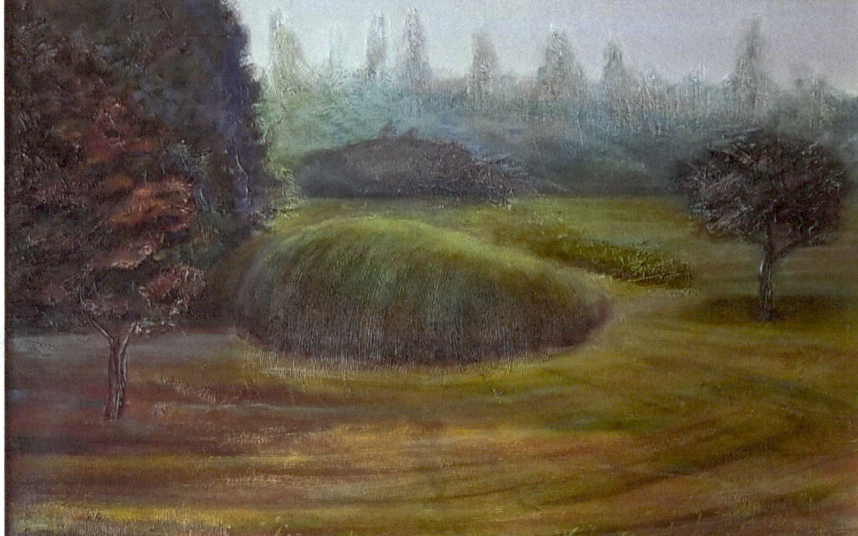
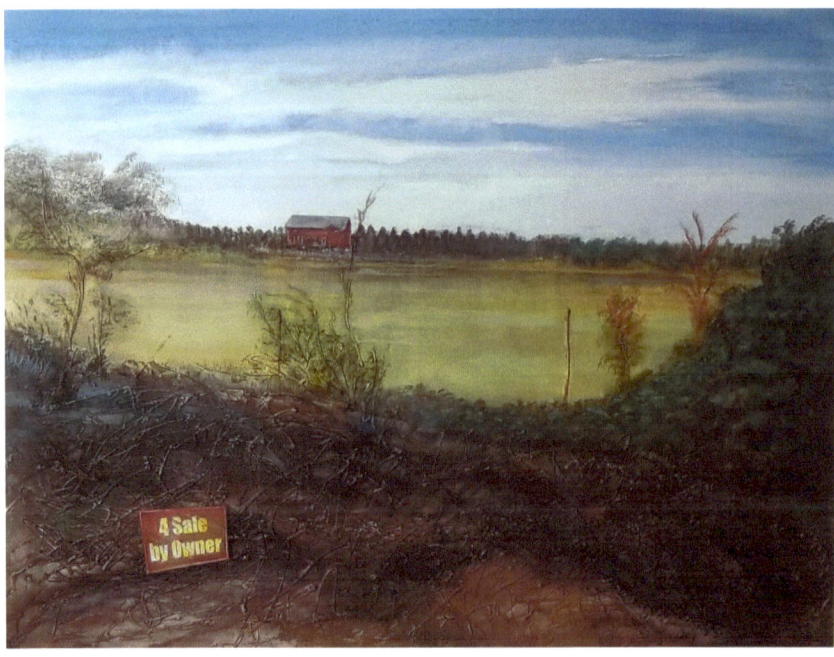
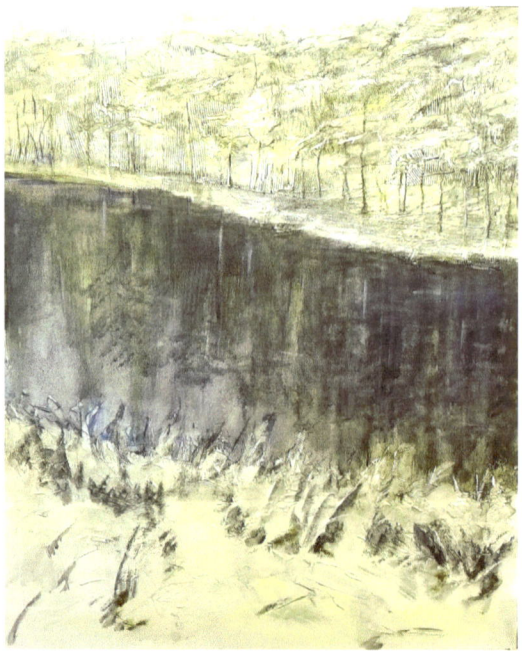

WWW.GARDEAVANT.ORG — APRIL 6 - 8, 2018

International Salon of Contemporary Art

Luda Makarova-Popovich

"I love color. I use complex palette, strong brush strokes- broad but precise to construct space and form. It allows me to capture and bring out the essence of the subject rather than its details. I aim to paint the only essential elements contributing to the work. There is inner truth, harmony, beauty in all things. Apparently simple everyday objects are visually complex. Need to capture and to share this beautiful complexity is my motivation to paint.

When I perceive new line or color I fall in love with it. I study this impression over and over to feel intricate relationships of the subjects. Their form and function, certain shapes, textures and colors, the way light falls. That's the hardest part of all. Then it's easy - just to transfer the image on the canvas. And at last- the longest and intense part- to get it right. Compositions have their own logic that dictates necessary changes. My best works are like generators. They live by themselves. Every time I look at them they give me new feelings and ideas.

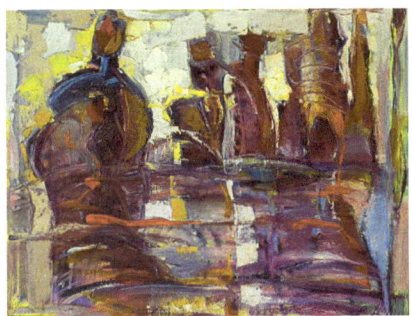

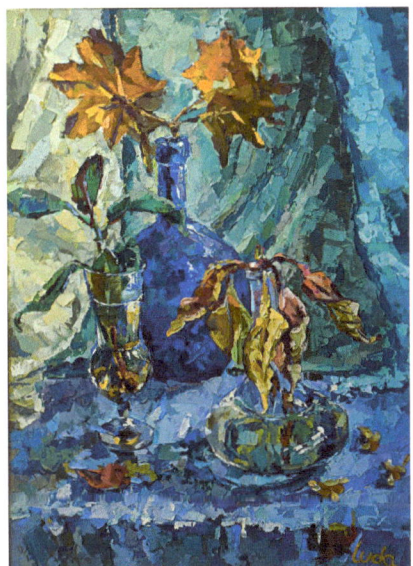

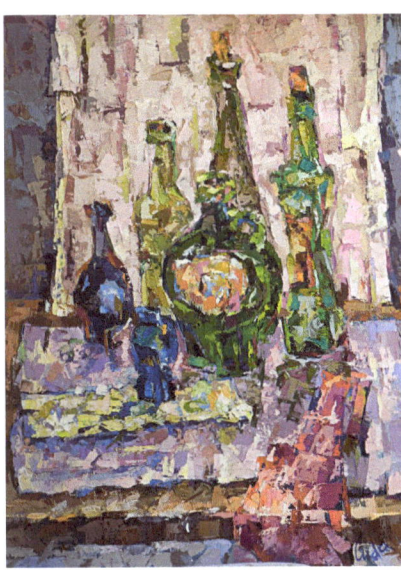

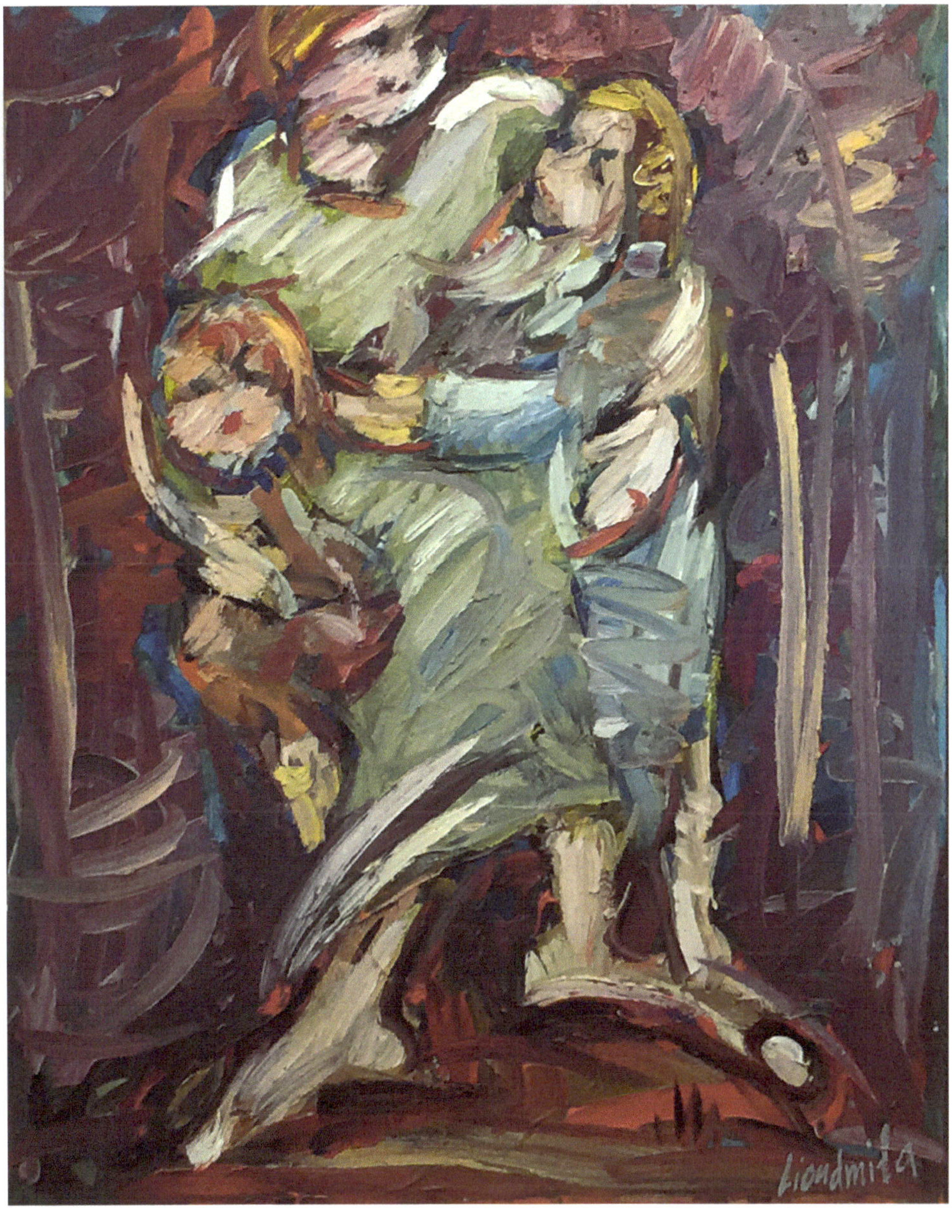

www.GardeAvant.org

APRIL 6 - 8, 2018

INTERNATIONAL SALON OF CONTEMPORARY ART

Elena Dobrovolskaya

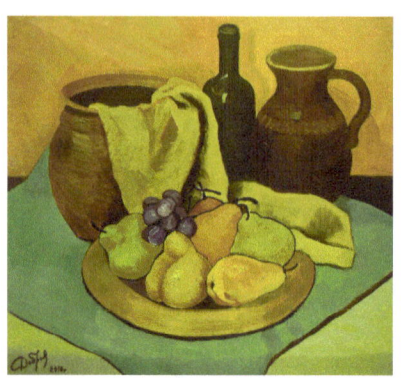

Elena Dobrovolskaya was drawn to art from her early years, but the path to becoming an oil painter has not been a straight one. Despite studying drawing during school years, she decided to follow in her mother's footsteps and graduated with a degree in chemical engineering.

Her career soon turned to business - she founded a travel company. 15 years in travel business gave Elena a unique opportunity to visit the best art museums in the world and to study art history from the original works of the great masters.

Elena radically changed her life in 2010 – she closed her business and returned to her passion for art. She took up private lessons of oil painting with renowned artist Oleg Leonov, a bright member of the Russian Academy of Art, famous for his realistic portraits and landscapes.

From her teacher she captured a Russian school technique of Old Masters and added her own vision of classical portraiture with a bright, tasteful color palette. After only a year at Leonov's art studio Elena Dobrovolskaya became a member of the Creative Union of Russia's Artists.

In 2011-2012 she worked as a curator of large-scale photo exhibitions in New York, Moscow, Paris and Strasbourg.

In 2012 Elena moved to the US. She lives and works at her art studio in Westchester, NY.

www.elenadobrovolskaya.com

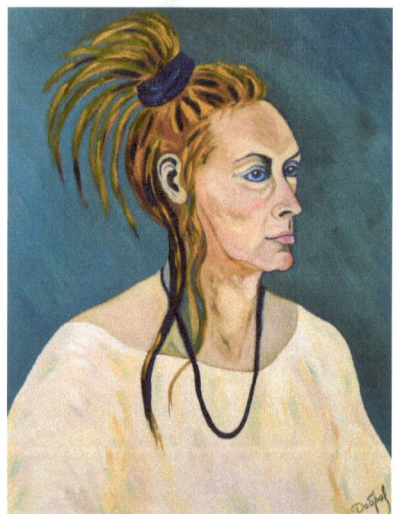

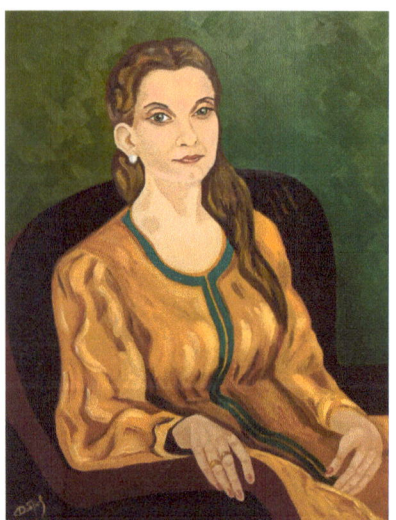

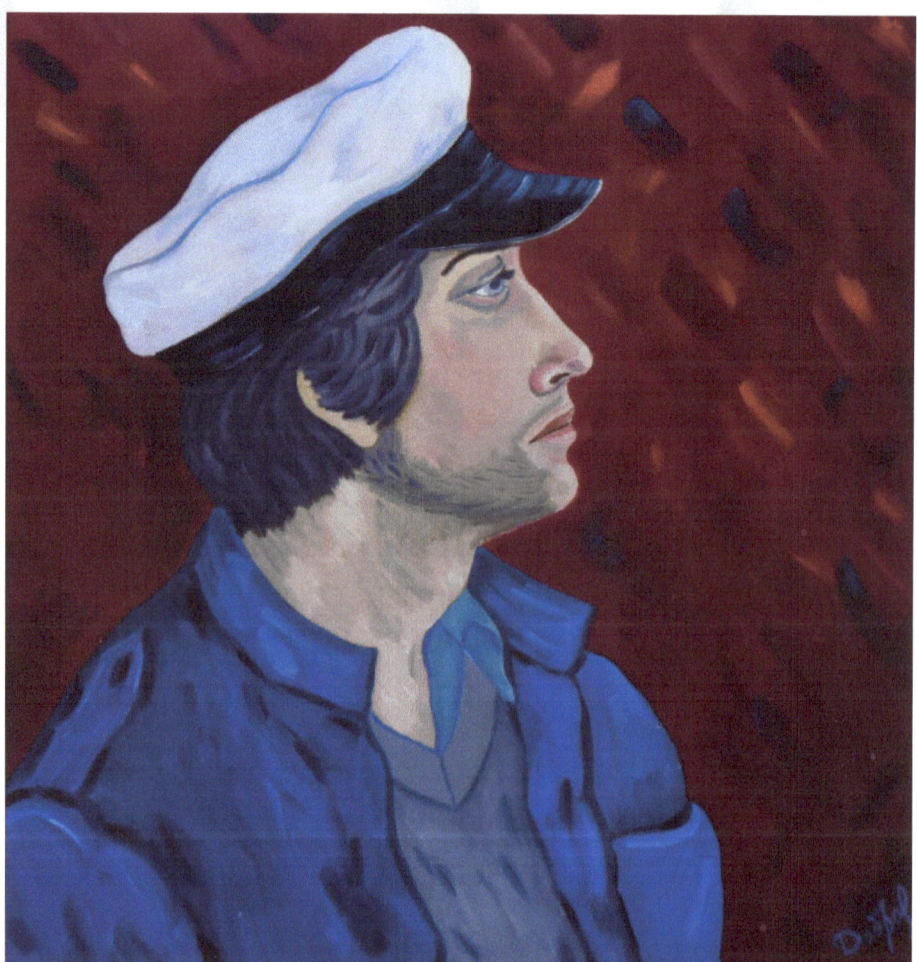

WWW.GARDEAVANT.ORG

APRIL 6 - 8, 2018

INTERNATIONAL SALON OF CONTEMPORARY ART

Leo Hanian

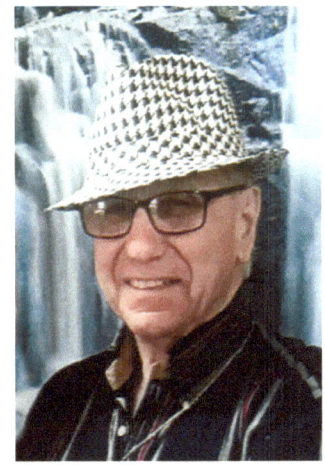

Born in Baku, Azerbaijan, (former USSR) in October 13, 1942. Graduated art collage, worked with art foundation. Participated in art exhibitions in Baku and Moscow. 1984 – member of the commonwealth of artists of the USSR. Emigrated in the USA in 1990, worked as a sculptor. Author of four large monuments in Philadelphia and Saint Louis. One of the monuments, placed in Shalom Memorial Park, is dedicated to the Jews, killed in Babiy Yar (Kiev). Participated in exhibition held in Philadelphia Gallery.

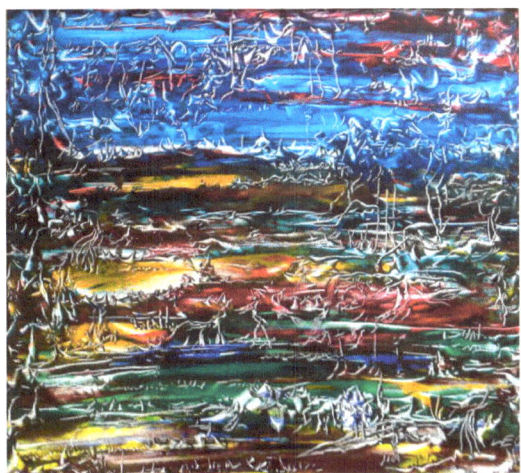
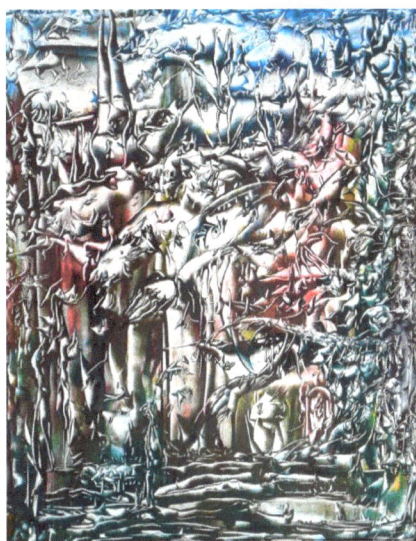
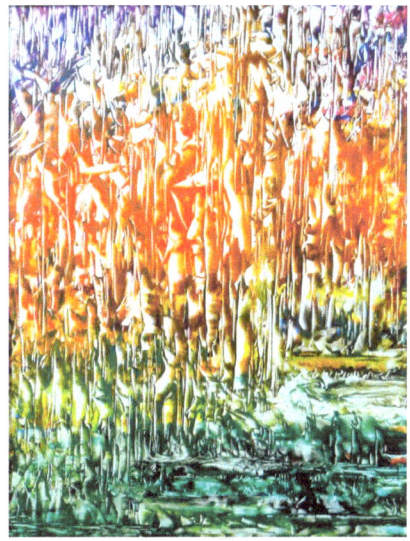

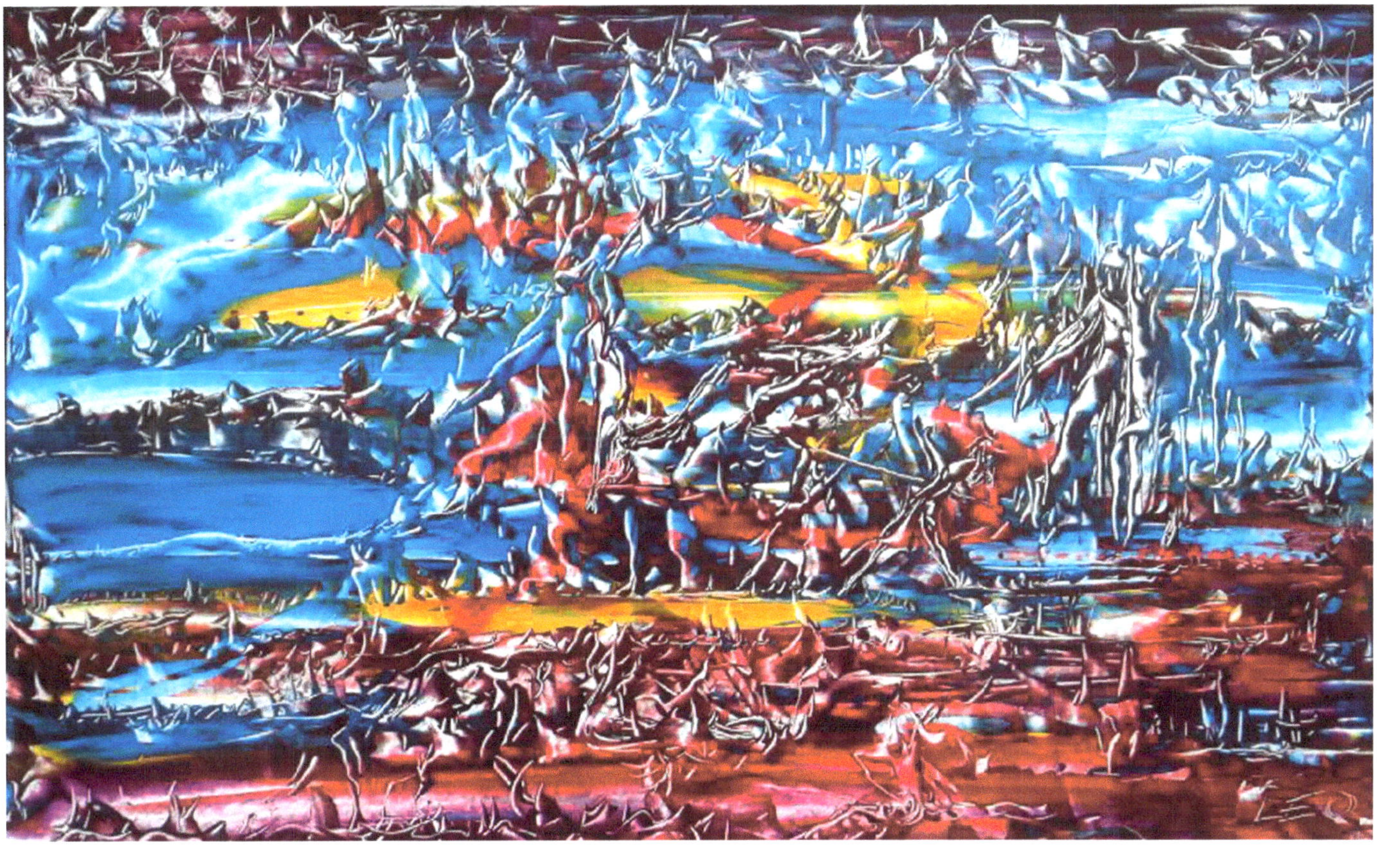

WWW.GARDEAVANT.ORG

APRIL 6 - 8, 2018

International Salon of Contemporary Art

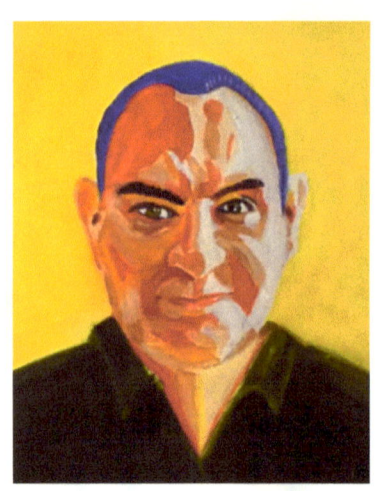

Aleksandr E. Kushner

The artist and writer Aleksandr E Kushner was born in Leningrad, now Saint Petersburg, Russia. As long as he remembers, he always drew, starting from the war years of the Second World War. The first watercolor paints were from half-used cardboard boxes, exchanged for a week's ratio of bread issued during the war.

The personal exhibition of Aleksandr E Kushner was held only in 1995. Since 1996 he has lived and worked in Colorado. He is a member of the Boulder Art Association.

He works mainly in the style of expressionism, expressing not the actual reality, but mainly the emotional state of the author. He has remained faithful to this style from the 1960's, when he began his struggle against the formalist forms and closeness of Russian society.

The portrait painting of Aleksandr E Kushner is mostly realistic. The works of Aleksandr E Kushner are kept in private collections in the USA, Russia, France, England, Hungary, Finland and Japan.

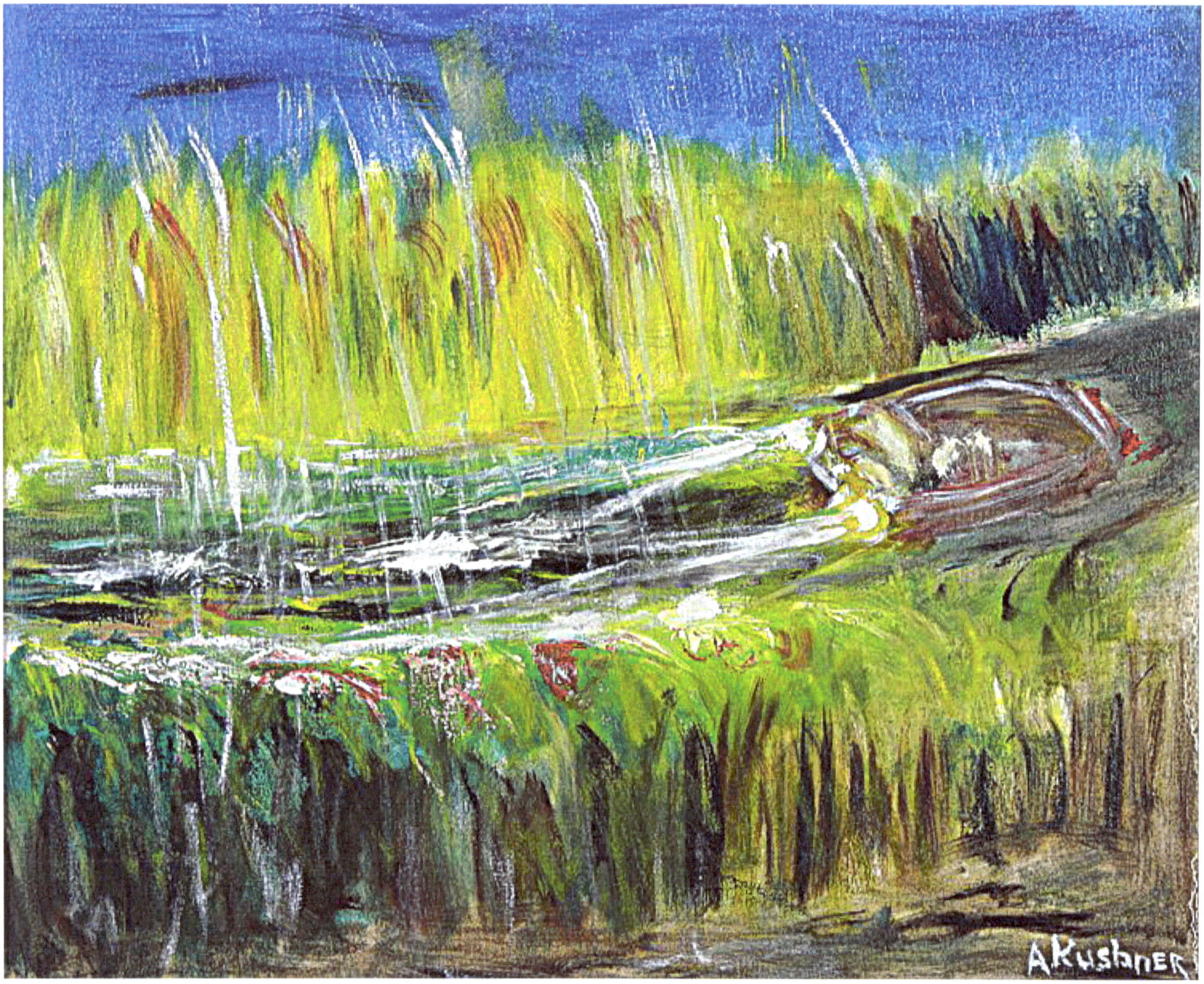

WWW.GARDEAVANT.ORG — APRIL 6 - 8, 2018

INTERNATIONAL SALON OF CONTEMPORARY ART

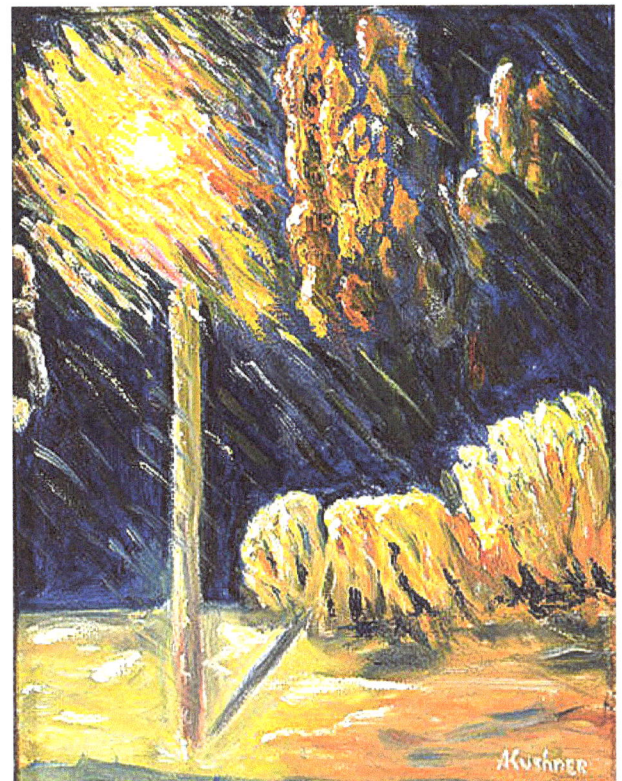
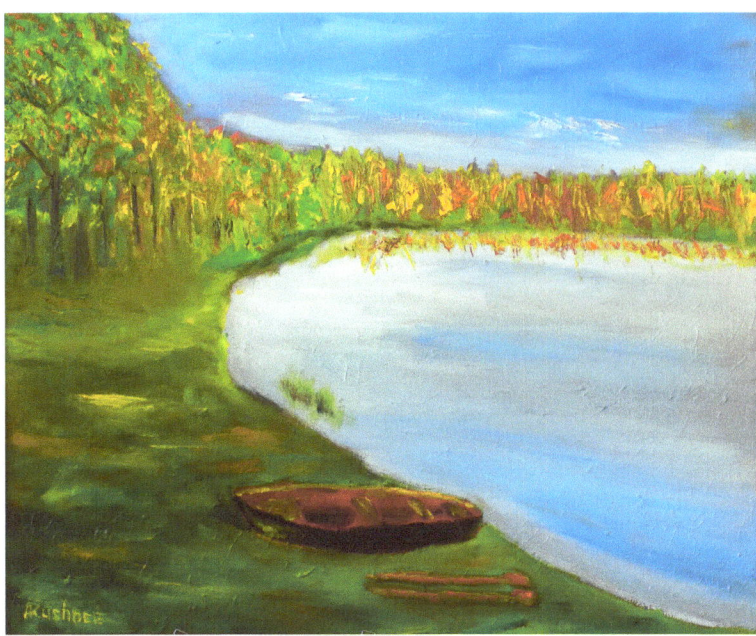
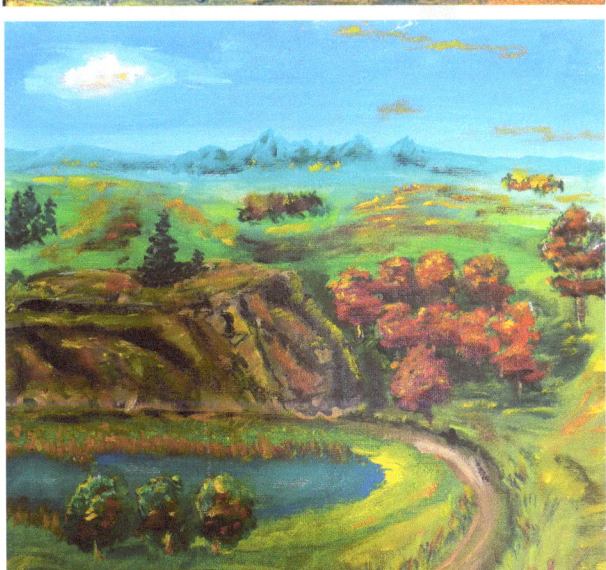
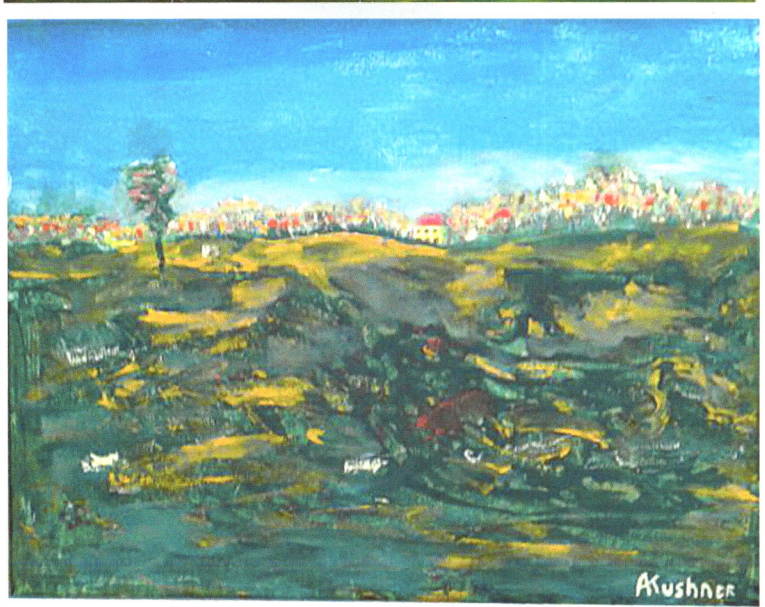
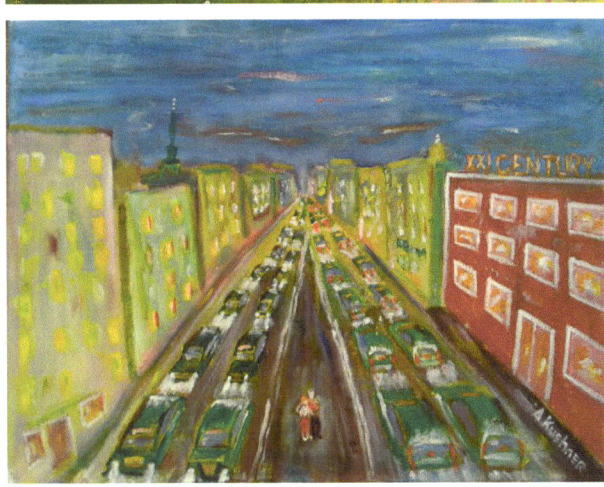
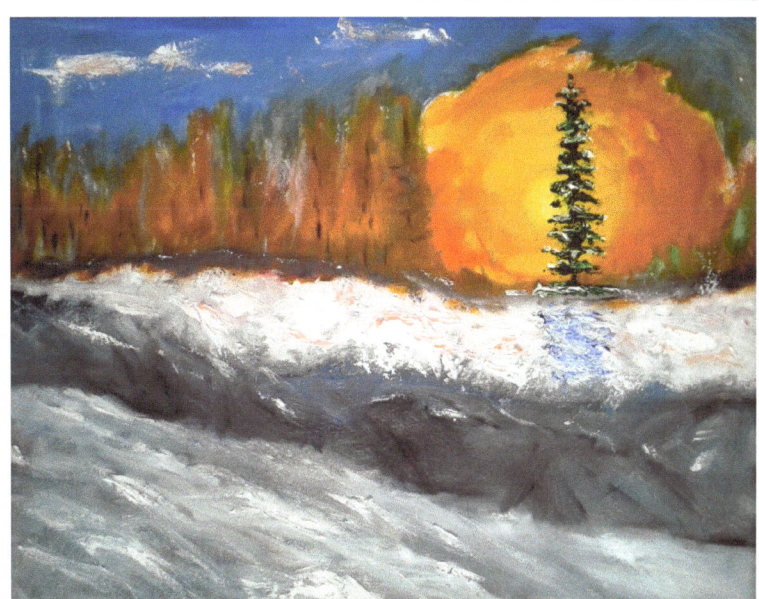

WWW.GARDEAVANT.ORG   APRIL 6 - 8, 2018

INTERNATIONAL SALON OF CONTEMPORARY ART

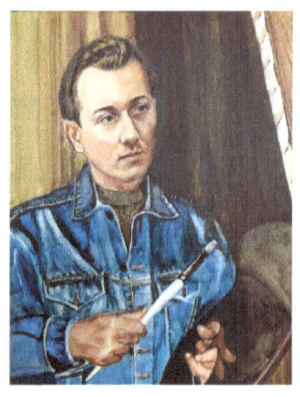

Isaak Fishkis

I had the luck of being born in Odessa, Ukraine. Odessa is a warm southern town by the picturesque shores of the Black Sea. My early days there were a time of kind Jewish traditions, art, best theater in the country and an endless number of talented, warm and funny people. It didn't take long for me to fall in love with this beauty around me and art was the outlet for my appreciation of it.

My love for art started around 5th Grade. All of my notebooks were covered in colorful sketches of flowers, blooming trees, birds in flight and anything I thought was beautiful. Until I discovered a different kind of beauty, the female form. This started my love for portraits and none were happier than the female subjects in these portraits.

After high school I completed the Art Institute of Grekov.

I saw beauty in everything around me and in my search for the right colors and lines to describe the beauty in my mind my art became the meaning of life for me and the path to beauty.

My second degree was in Electrical Engineering, but my love and interest in art and sculpture never dissipated and always remained ja part of my life.

Painter Isaac B. Fishkis, March 2018

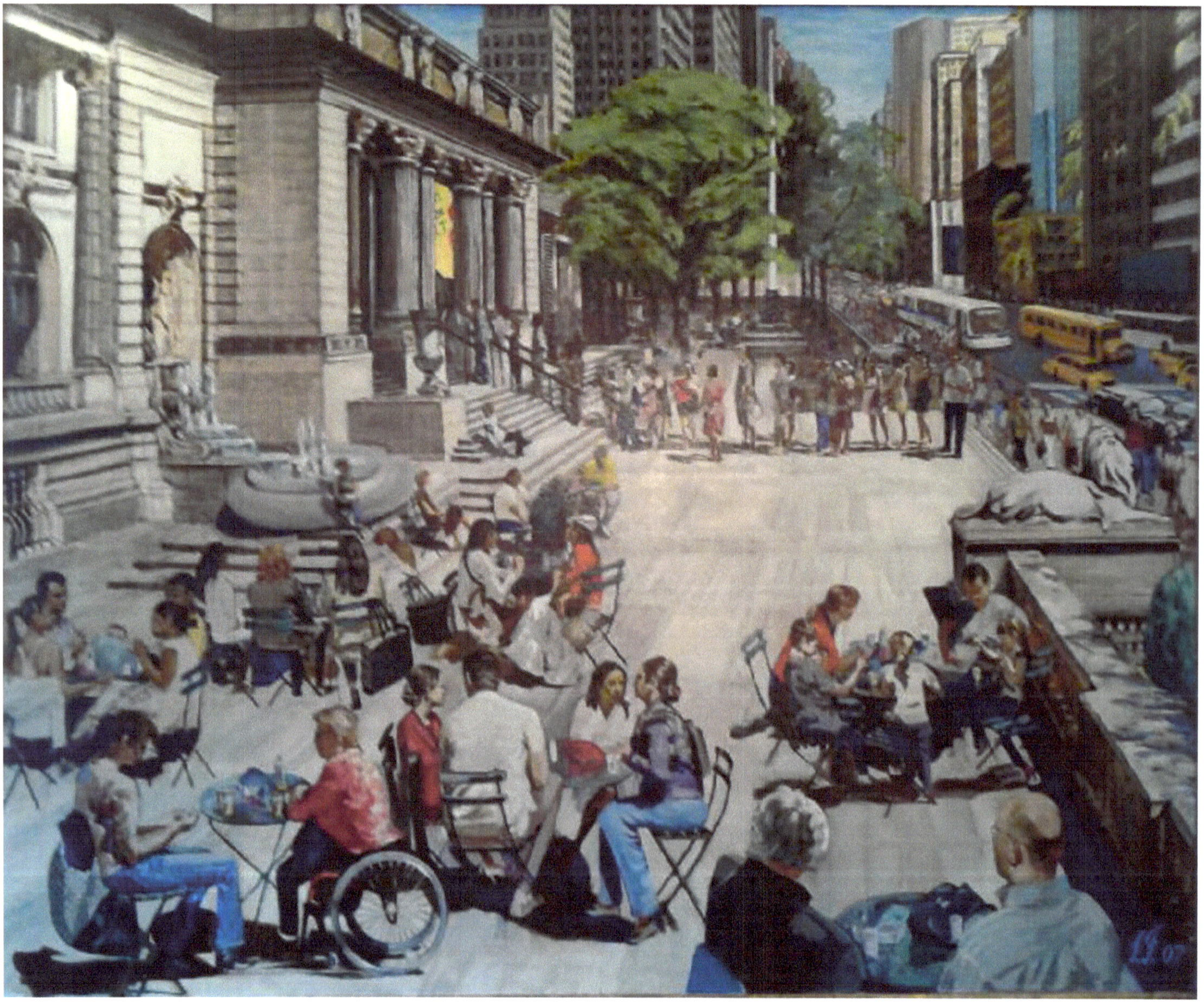

WWW.GARDEAVANT.ORG APRIL 6 - 8, 2018

International Salon of Contemporary Art

Isaak Fishkis

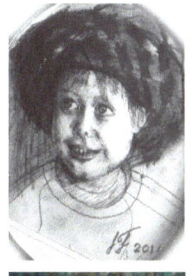
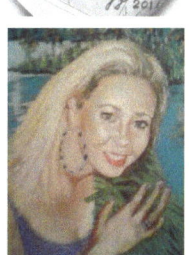
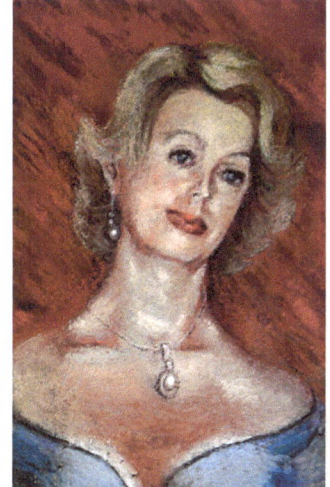
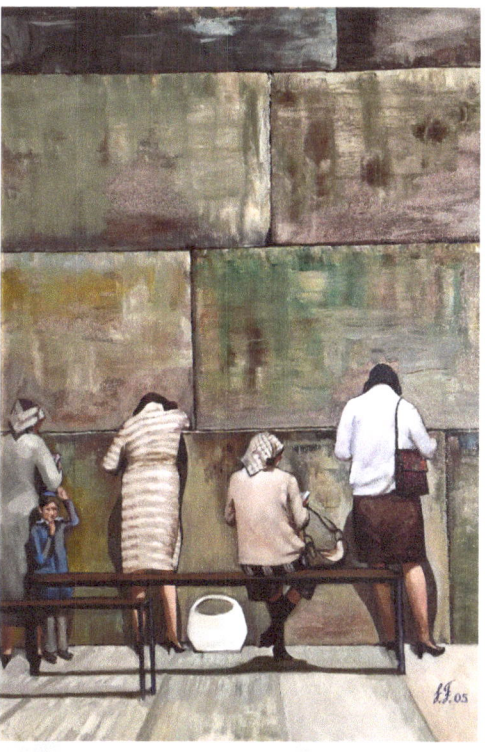

Women at Western Wall. Jerusalem.

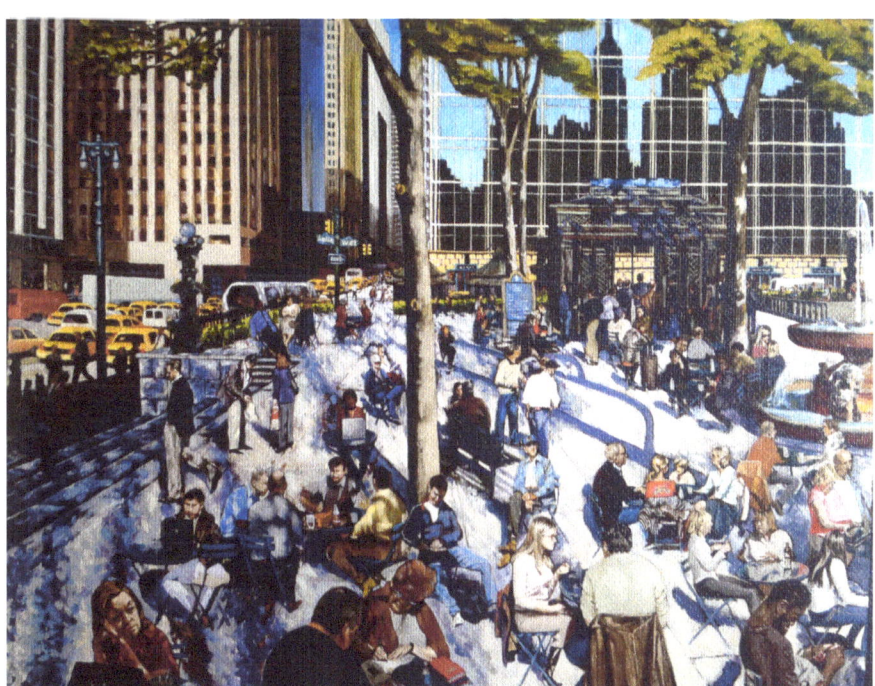
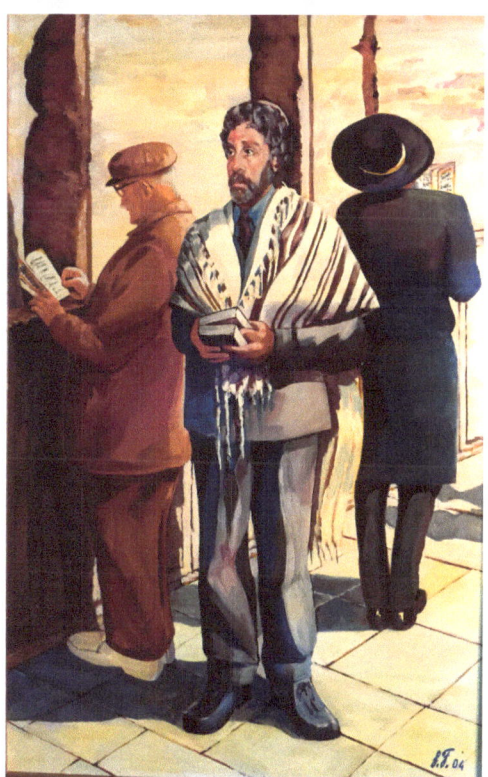

Thousands years we are reading, praying and struggling. Western Wall, Jerusalem.

WWW.GARDEAVANT.ORG   APRIL 6 - 8, 2018

INTERNATIONAL SALON OF CONTEMPORARY ART

Lev Brodsky

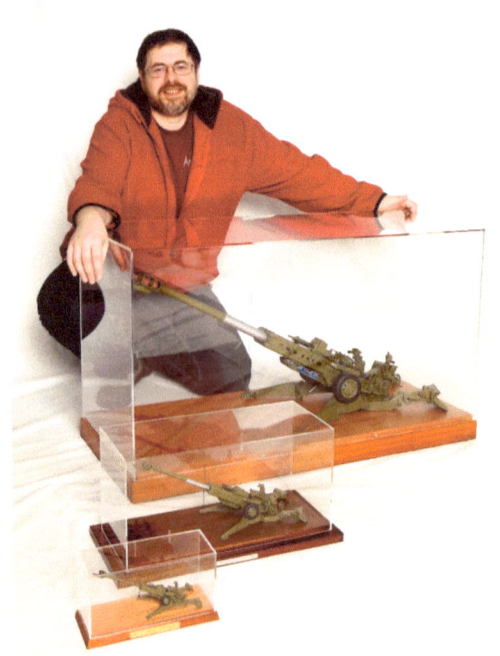

was born in 1963 in Moscow.

He is a professional model maker, sculptor, toys and collectibles designer. Most of his works are commissioned by various companies, including renown toy and collectibles manufacturers such as Danbury Mint, Franklin Mint, Mattel and Hasbro.

Lev Brodsky lives in Philadelphia, Pennsylvania.

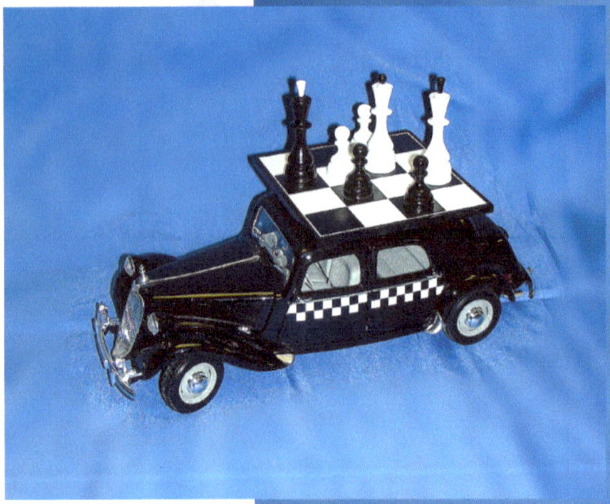

Chessmobile
mixed media

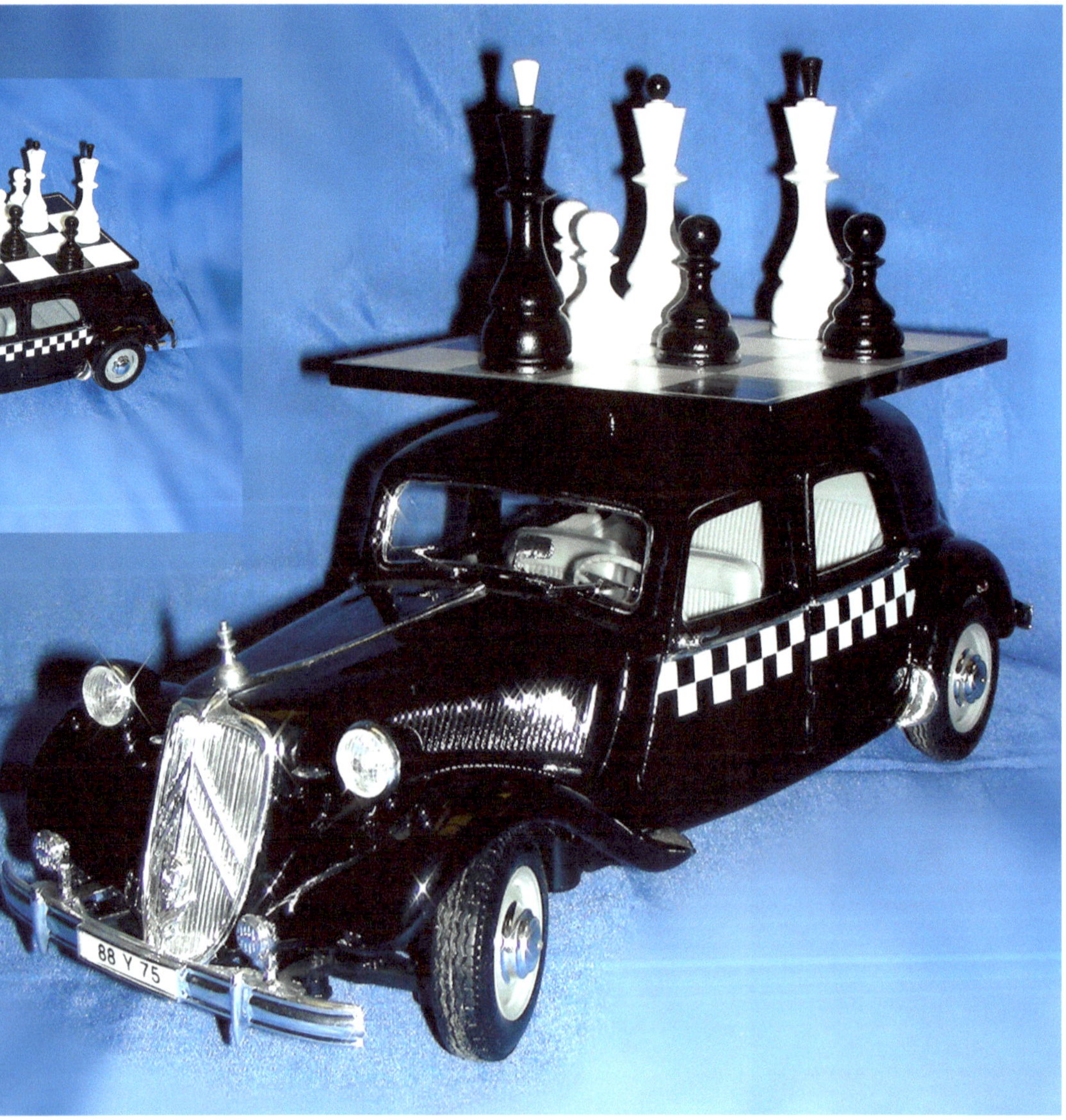

WWW.GARDEAVANT.ORG

APRIL 6 - 8, 2018

INTERNATIONAL SALON OF CONTEMPORARY ART

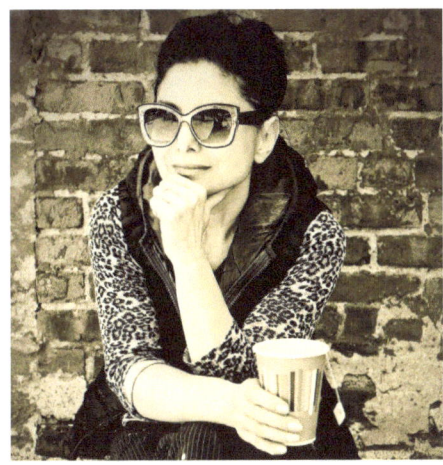

Kora Velikhanly

Painter, Sculptor
Scenic artist, mural artist....

"The Artist is not someone who just creates in an artistic fashion. It is a state of mind, and love. A person who percieves the world in a very special and unique way."

- Member of United Scenic Artists union, local USA 829, also known as United Scenic Artists of America

- The members of Local USA 829 are Artists and Designers working in film, theatre, opera, ballet, television, industrial shows, commercials and exhibitions

"Art and love are the same thing: It's the process of seeing yourself in things that are not you."
            Chuck Klosterman

- Member of SAG-AFTRA union. Screen Actors Guild American Federation of Television and Radio Artists.

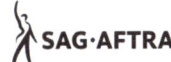

"The purpose of art is washing the dust of daily life off our souls"
            Pablo Picasso.

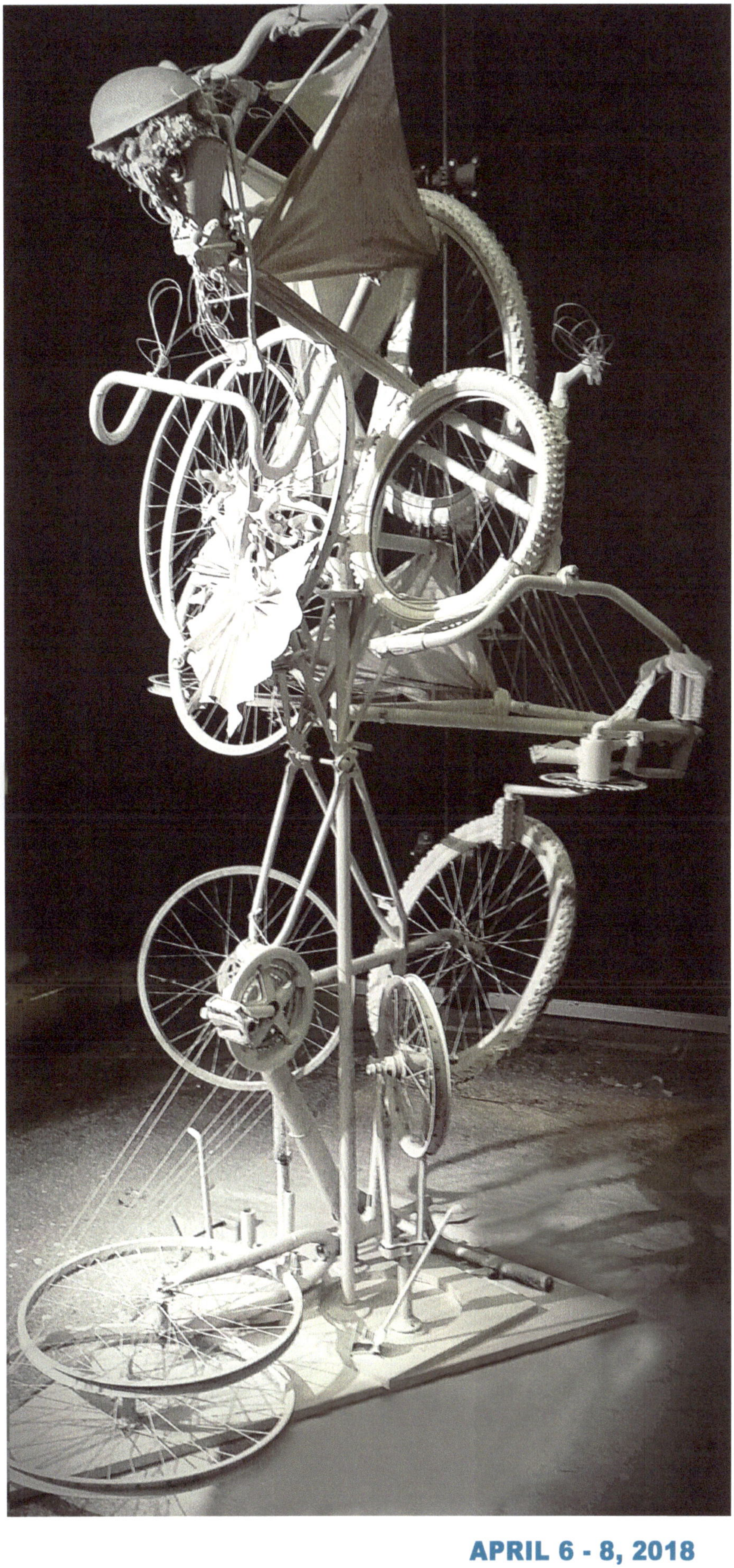

WWW.GARDEAVANT.ORG

APRIL 6 - 8, 2018

INTERNATIONAL SALON OF CONTEMPORARY ART

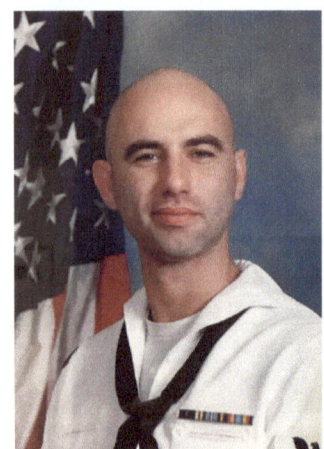

Vladislav Rudkin

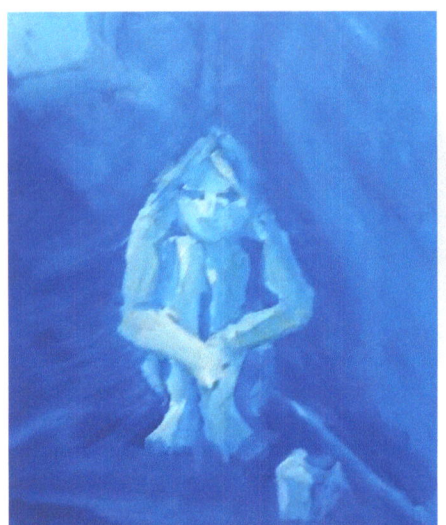

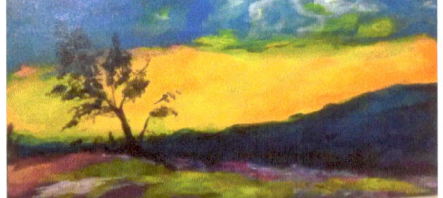

I Vladislav Rudkin was born in beautiful city by the sea Odessa. Family – working class, mother; nurse practitioner, father- welding inspector, and latter little sister charming creature. Early biography is nothing enchanted; "Free audient "and "Bright head" that how teachers call me before my parents when they were called to visit school. Somewhere at that time I was introduced to rock`n`roll, which accompany me since through my adventures life. Then was college which I left during my first year to get a haircut. That gives me an idea; since I don't need haircut anymore, maybe I should go back? Sometimes I had to work, that was and still idea of life for majority people around me. So I did work during brief periods between care free lives with my friends. As good student on September 1st of 1993 I opened new "Bookvar` "- it was in English. I tried to be productive member of society, only I didn't see how it can benefit me, and what is it exactly society produce? But money is a necessity, just for simple reason as to support ones habits. Once upon a time I stumble on add in newspaper "firefighting training", so I called. Voice in the phone inform me that such training available and provided by US NAVY, but in order to receive it I have to join it. My romantic nature of boy from Black Sea responded: "Where do I sign?". Soon I became United States Sailor. On board USS STOUT I did 2 tours in Persian Gulf. Visit few countries, saved few ships, took few pictures. After 4 and ½ years honorably discharged and came to New York to visit my sister. Still visiting. Here and there. Up and down. North and south. Not much east and west anymore. Life became routine and it's difficult to find something worth living for. Art gives me hope that if someone like what I do, maybe it's not so bad after all. As children we all pain and draw and do some other silly things that we are doing less and less as we grow up. I didn't. Well unfortunately I do less silly things. For my introduction to art I probably have to thank my father who was collecting post cards with reproductions of paintings by classic artists. Majority of my favorite artist formed then; education of Busch, passion of Goya, precision of Durer, colors of El Greco, later came imagination of Dali, simplicity of Picasso, grace of Degas. By the way Degas said: "Art is not to show people what you see, it is to show people what they what to see", I find it helpful when I try to bring out something in my work.

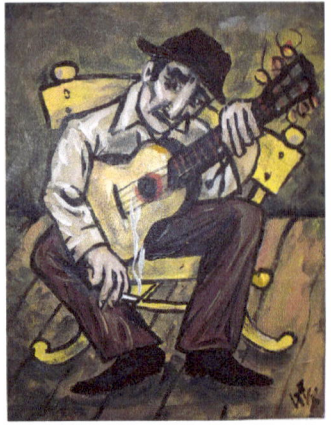
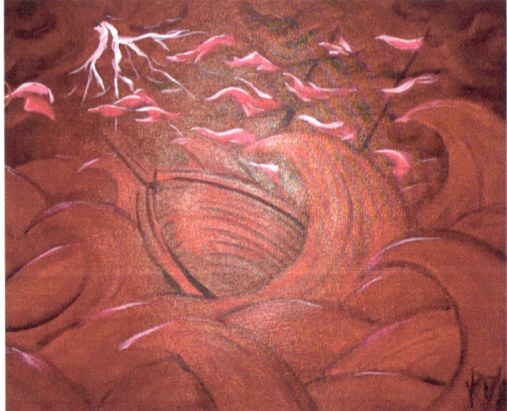
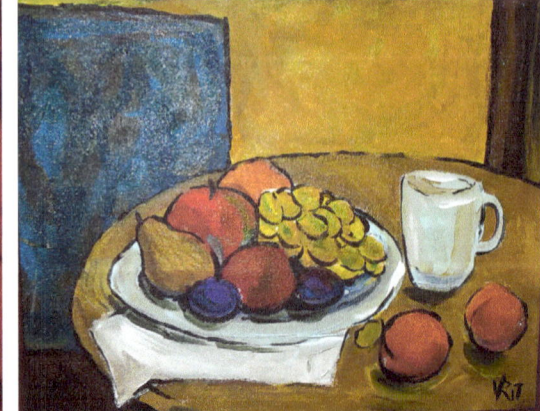

WWW.GARDEAVANT.ORG

APRIL 6 - 8, 2018

International Salon of Contemporary Art

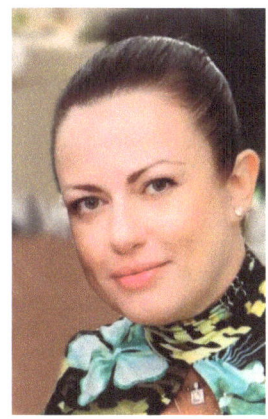

Lana Vain

Often parents put their children drawings on refrigerator. Not sure if it is size of our refrigerator, lack of magnets, or size of our ambitions, but for my sister and me it wasn't enough. We naturally need more. So once in the while we played "museum". We would paint pictures and post them around the room; our parents would walk around, look, talk, ask questions, and in the end, buy them. My sister Lana is very interesting person. She was born few years later in the same nursery as I. And her first breath was warm, fragrant, poetic and romantic (a little salty) breeze of beautiful Odessa. This breath stays with odessit for the rest of life; it's grow inside and often become beautiful flower. Not sure what caused for Lana to take brash deep it into paint and stand upfront of easel? But when she did, she unleashed her feelings, desire, and fantasy. Now happily married she live in Staten Island have three magnificent children, fluffy cat, and sometimes bunch of ladybugs. Kids, family, house and garden consume most of her time, but she still finding time to paint. Not as much and not as often a she would like. She dedicates majority of her time to show and teach kids beauty of colors, family, world. Her paintings are vibrant, bringing warm, dreamy and yet joyful feelings of summer. "The future belongs to those who believe in the beauty of their dreams." E. Roosevelt.

written by my brother Vladislav Rudkin

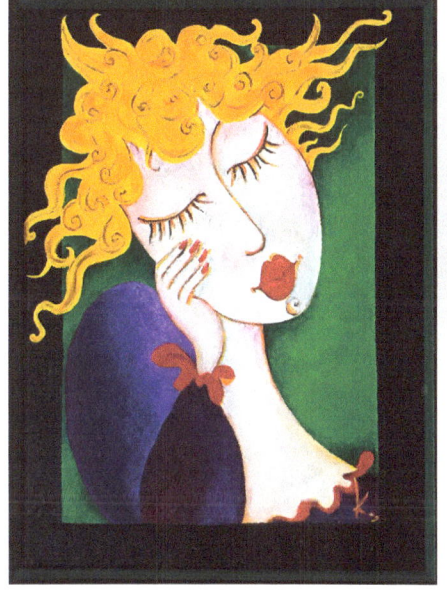
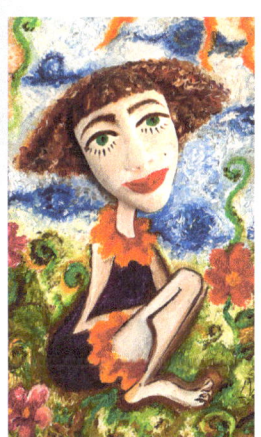
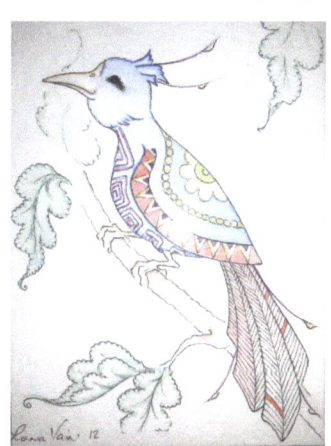
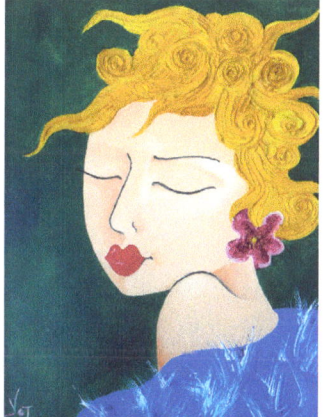
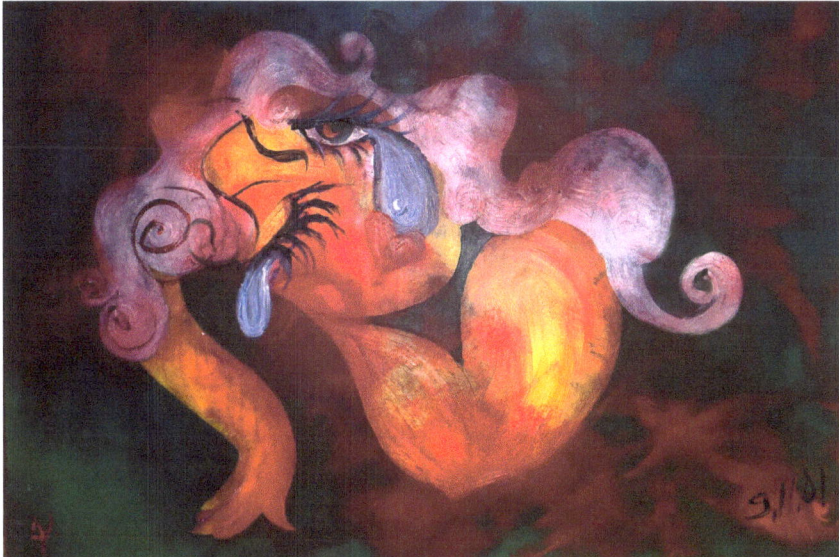
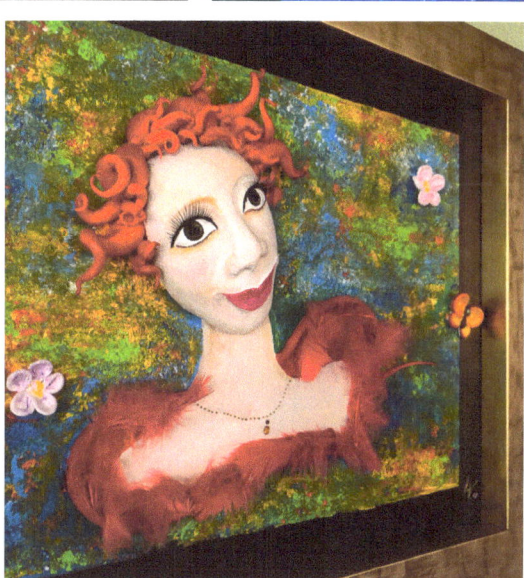

www.GardeAvant.org • April 6 - 8, 2018

INTERNATIONAL SALON OF CONTEMPORARY ART

Emanuel Antsis

"I don't know anything more mysterious and abstract than reality."

tel.: 267-423-7438
eantsis@gmail.com

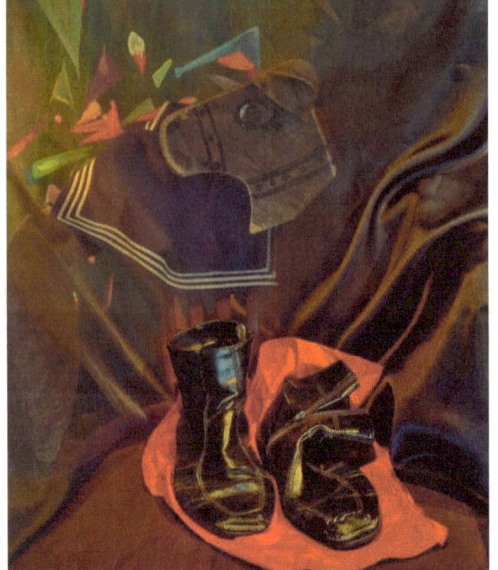
Boots of the prodigal son.

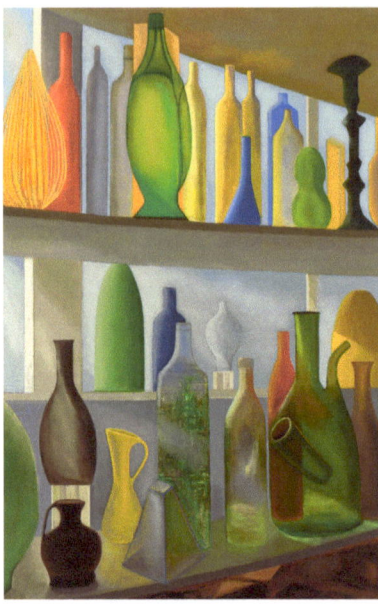
Light in my window.

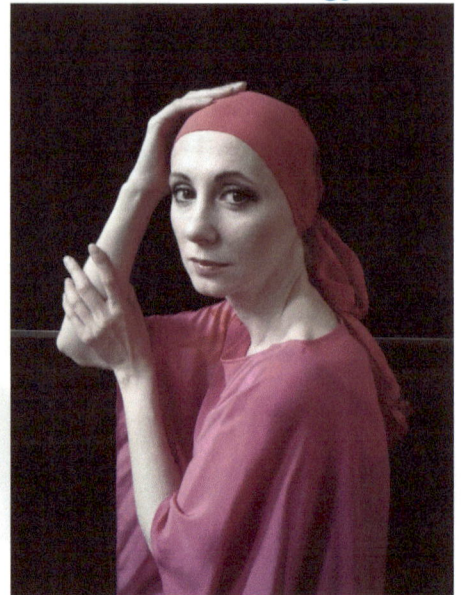
Valentina.

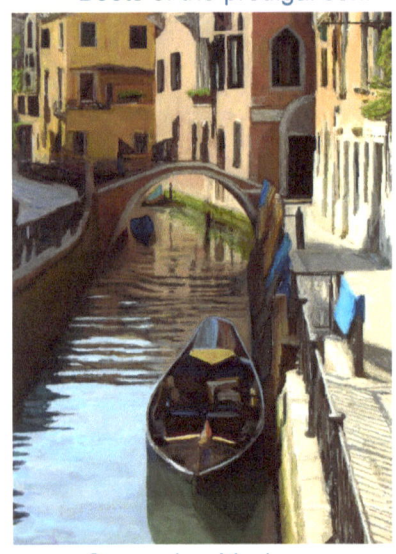
Sunny day. Venice.

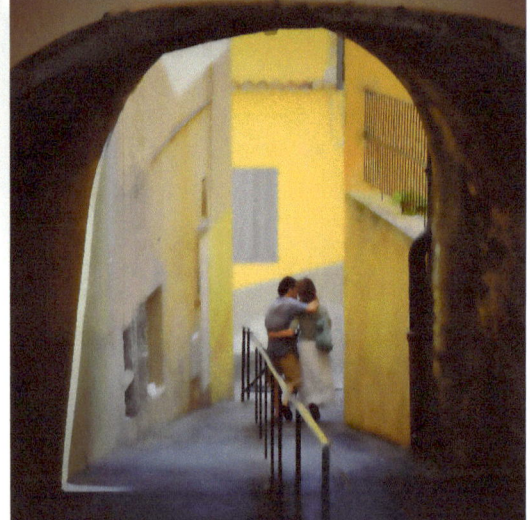
Love. France.

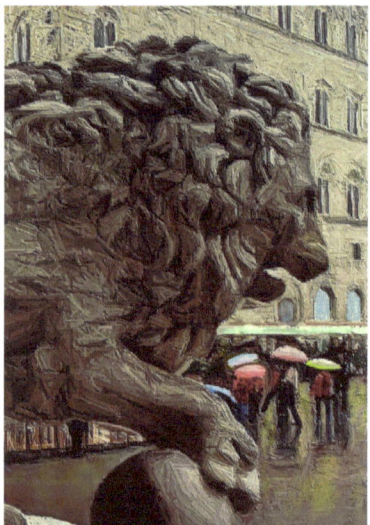
Florence.

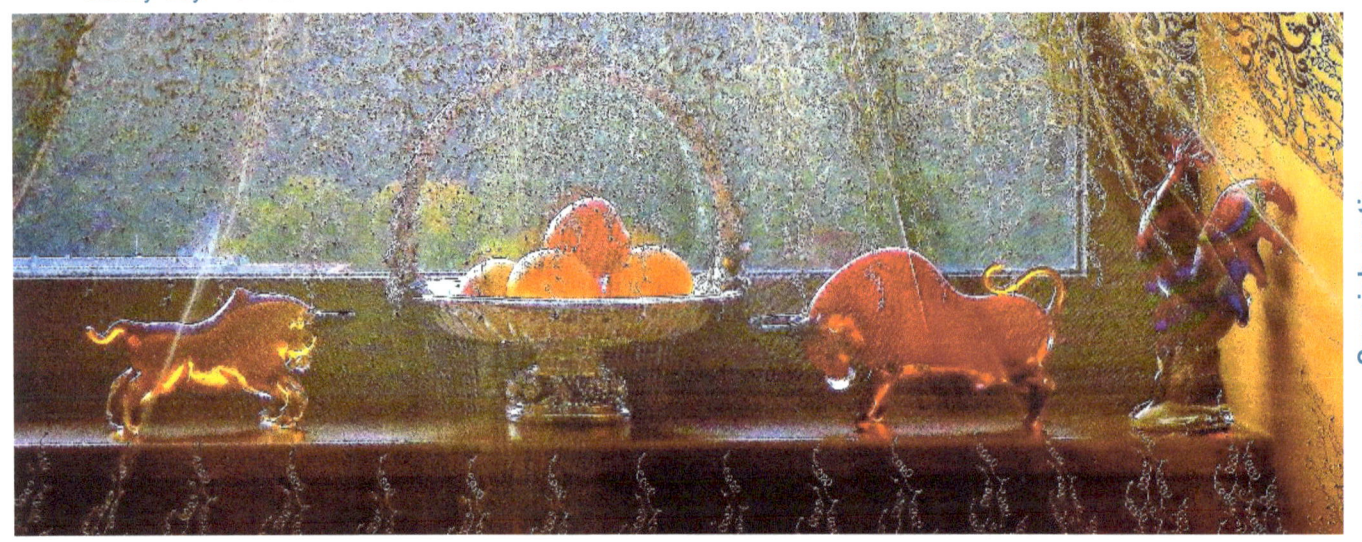
Spanish motiv.

WWW.GARDEAVANT.ORG

APRIL 6 - 8, 2018

INTERNATIONAL SALON OF CONTEMPORARY ART

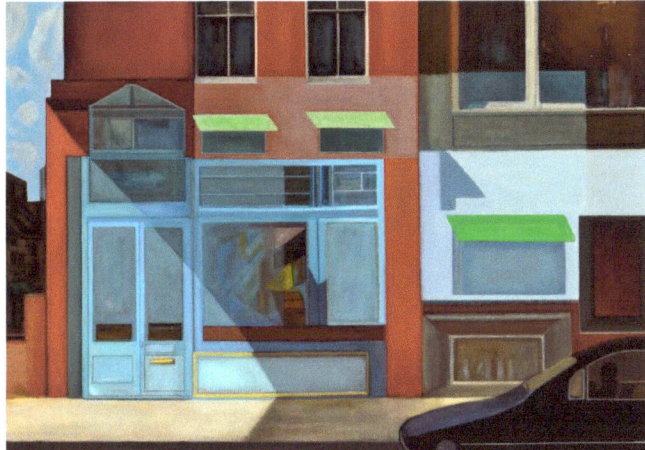
In honor of painter Edward Hopper.

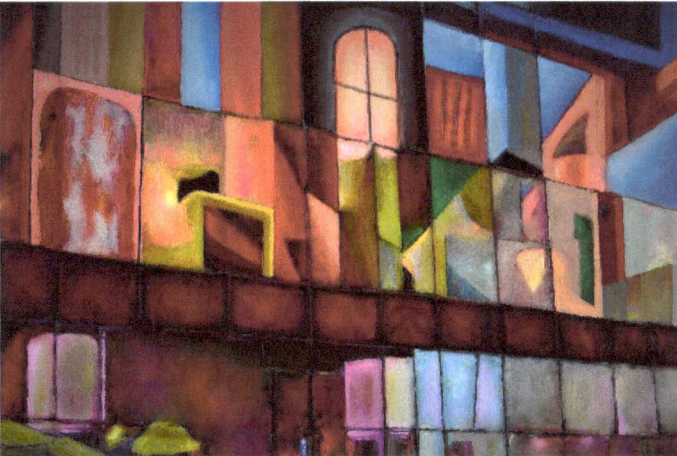
Palette of Time Square.

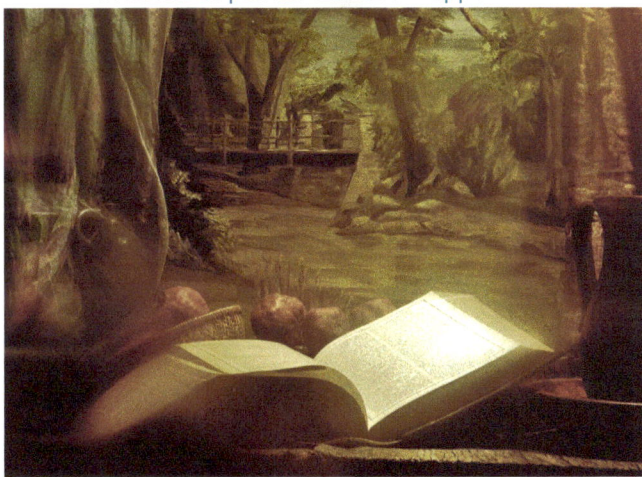
Old pages.

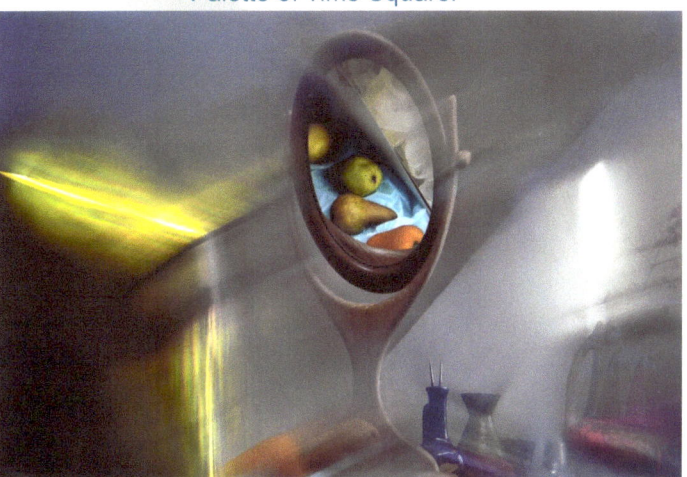
Mysterious light.

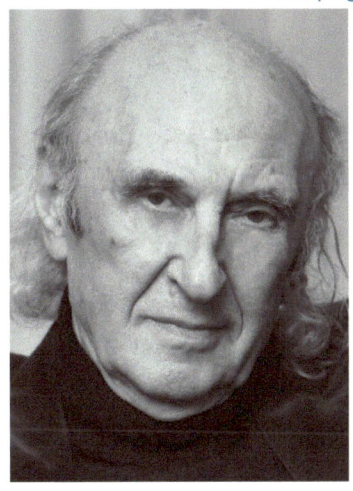

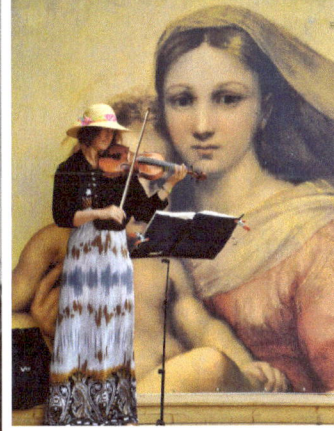
Music of Old Europe

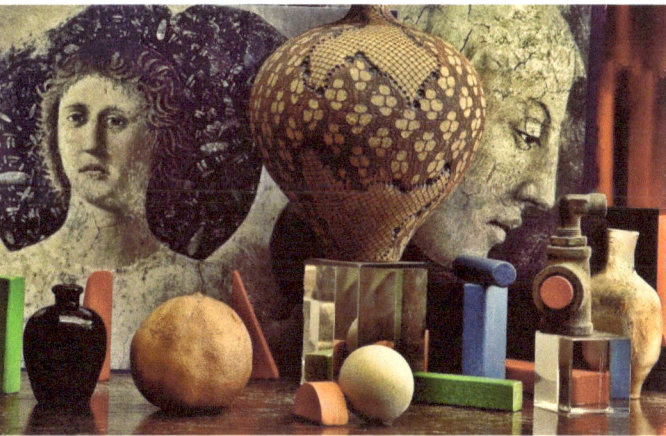
Time after time. Meeting epoch.

Emanuel Antsis was born in Kiev, Ukraine. Education: State Institute of Cinematography (Moscow). Field of activity: Filmmaking, Photography, Journalism. Film experience: 1962-1978 was working on Kiev Popular Science Film Studio. Shot more than 40 films, mostly as cameraman, some as director and screenwriter. Received numerous awards for some of his movies. The most known film "Computer and Riddle of Leonardo" - First Prize of Moscow Film Festival (1974), "Gold Shell" (Italy, 1975). Photographs and essays of Emanuel Antsis were published in numerous magazines and newspapers in Ukraine. In 1978 emigrated in USA. From 1980 had several personal exhibitions in USA and Canada: Print Club (Philadelphia) as winner of 1st place of international competition, in Science Center (Phila), gallery of Penn State University (Malvern). His photographs were published in bestseller book "Russia from inside" of American journalist Robert Kaiser and in "New American" (editor Sergey Dovlatov), essay "Look at the face" and novel "About Splendid Lady" in Novoe Russkoe Slovo - weekly Philadelphia. Some photographs of Emanuel Antsis were purchased for private collections and institutions.

WWW.GARDEAVANT.ORG   APRIL 6 - 8, 2018

INTERNATIONAL SALON OF CONTEMPORARY ART

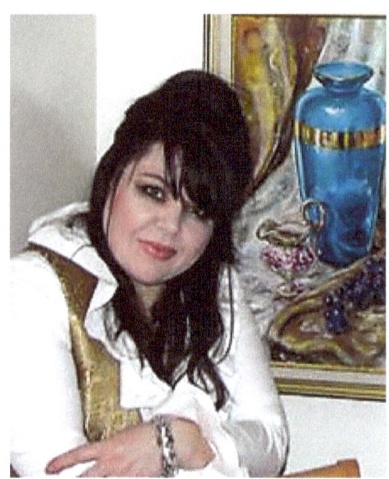

Diana Korobov

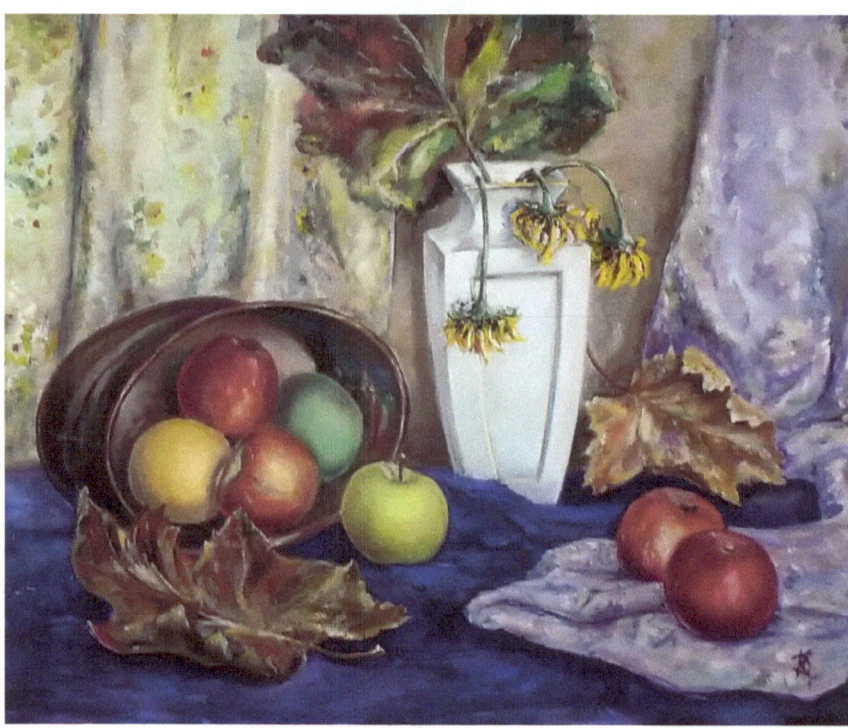

Born in Baku, Azerbaijan, Diana Korobov has been drawing and painting since childhood. At age seven, she had her first show in the hallway of the family apartment with pictures her grandfather saved of her early work. Ms. Korobov first studied art at the Pales of Pioneers in Baku and in high school won a city-wide art competition.

After college (major in Geology) in the 1990's Diana moved to Moscow, where she was drawing and painting and was frequently inspired by the city's great museums of art. In late 1995 she immigrated to the United States and continued her studies at Art Instruction School thru mail. Five years ago, she met her teacher Ludmila Makarova, well-known in Russian community of Philadelphia. Ms. Korobov went on studying at the Art Studio Palette oil and watercolor painting. Lately she interests to working in clay and creating pottery and sculpting figurine by polymer clay. Self-taught in graphics design, Ms. Korobov has created Websites for individuals and businesses.

Diana has shown and sold her works through shown at Art Studio Palette, Salon 191 and private showings. She and her husband reside in Northeast Philadelphia.

diana.korobov.com

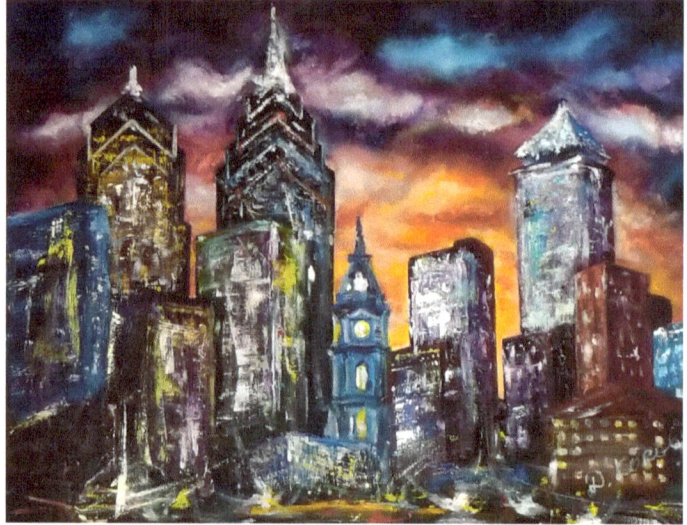

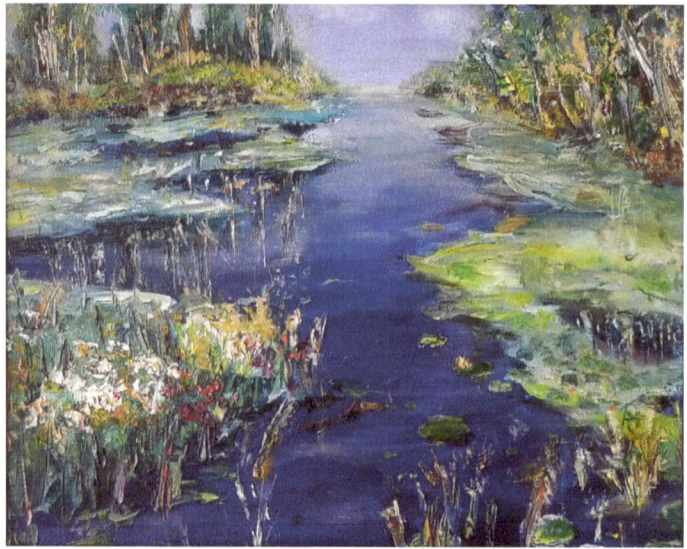

International Salon of Contemporary Art

Diana Korobov

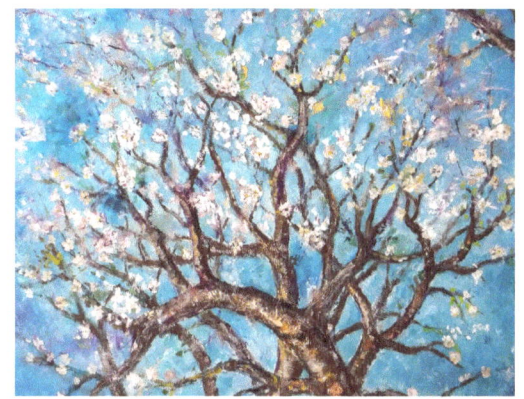
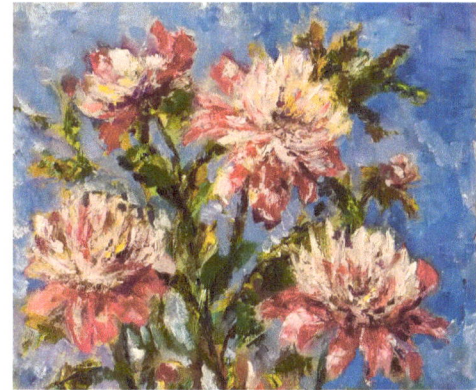
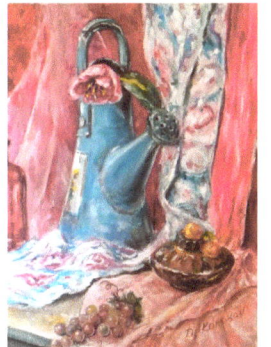
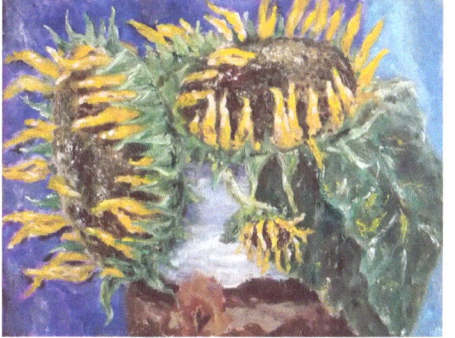
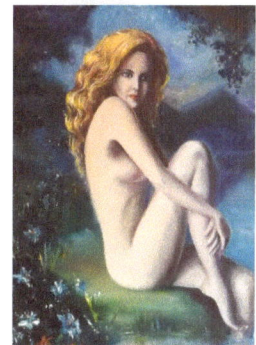
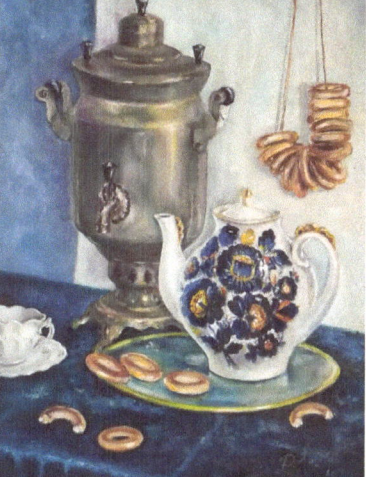
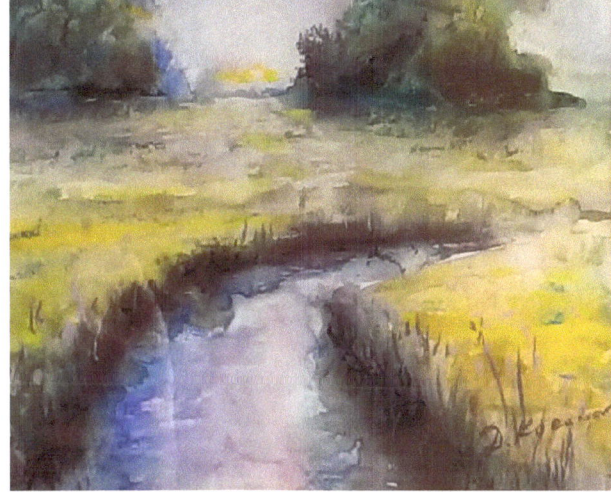
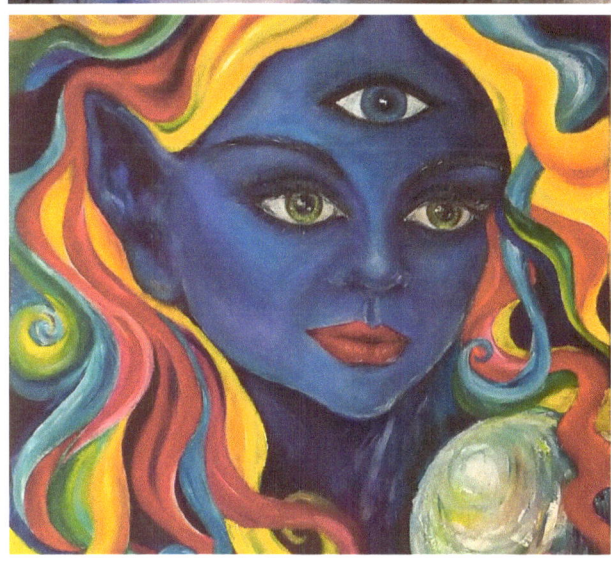
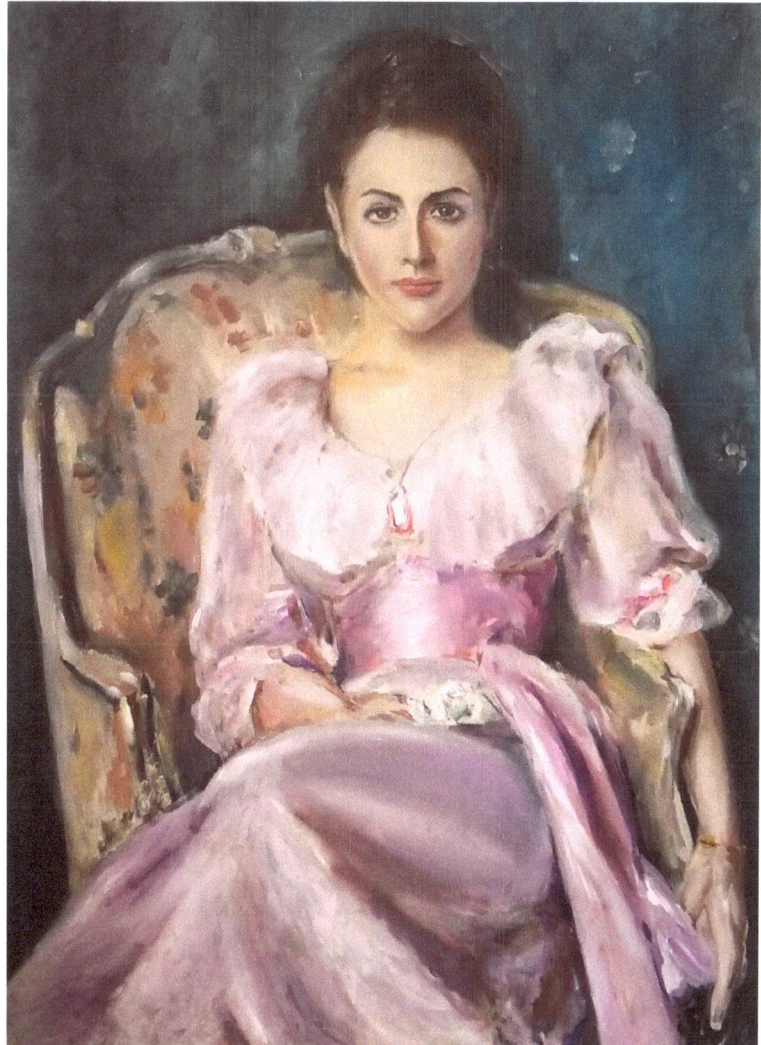

WWW.GARDEAVANT.ORG APRIL 6 - 8, 2018

International Salon of Contemporary Art

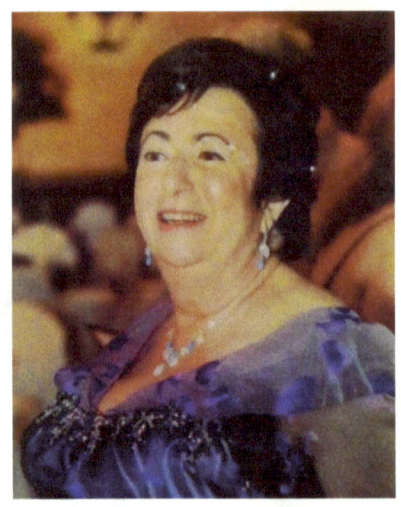

Sarra Rudkin-Peysakh

I am Sarra Rudkina-Peysakh, was born and raised in Odessa, Ukraine. I worked my whole life as a nurse in the policlinics, in emergency room. I came to the United States in 1994 with my son and my daughter and now I have three beautiful grandchildren. My life path crossed with the path of Ludmila Makarova, the Artist and the Art Teacher. At that time, I decided to try myself in ceramics.

Once I used the paintbrush on canvas for the first time in my life. That beginning opened absolutely new world for me – the world of beautiful Colors. Since that moment I saw the world in different way, I want to draw everything around me. And I will. As I have the whole life ahead of me and many new paintings to come.

Sarra Rudkina-Peysakh

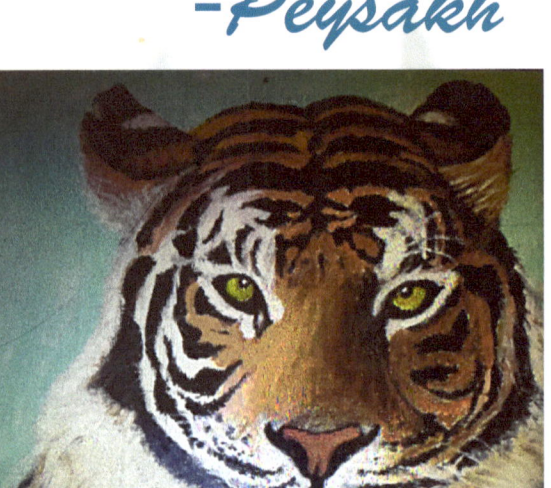

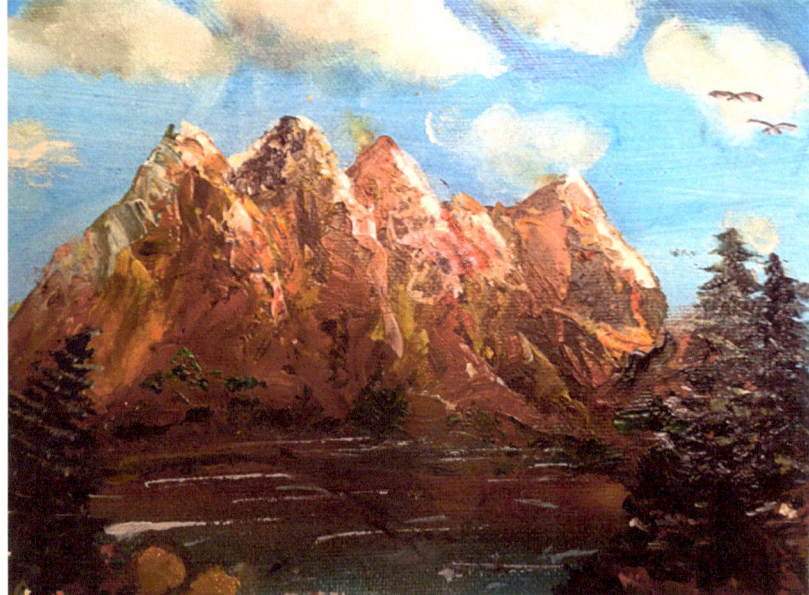

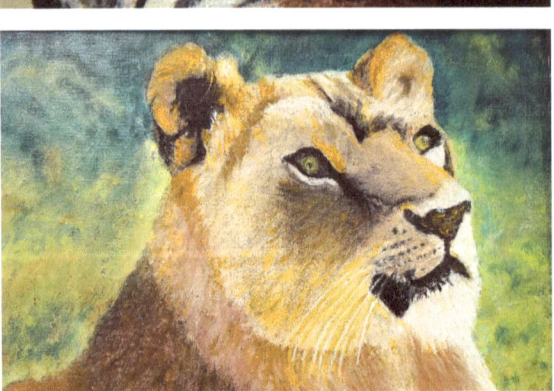

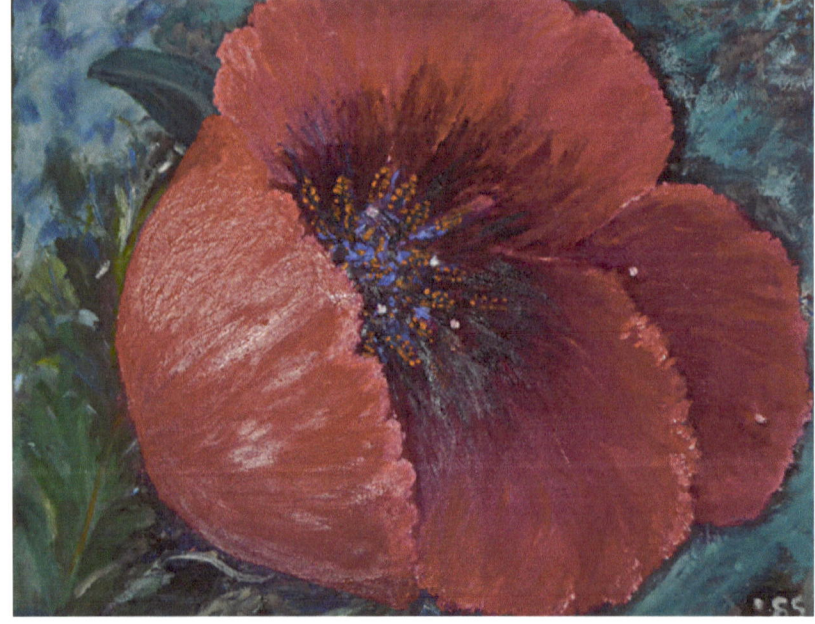

WWW.GARDEAVANT.ORG

APRIL 6 - 8, 2018

INTERNATIONAL SALON OF CONTEMPORARY ART

Tetiana Belkina

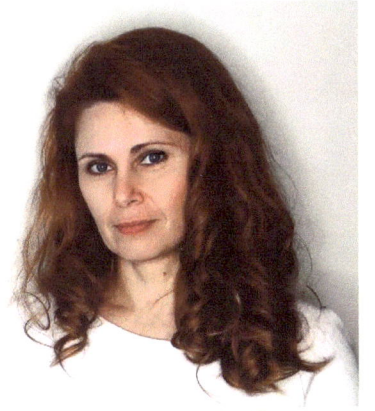

At the beginning painting was my hobby. I painted landscapes and learning how to paint in the process. One day I tried to paint a portrait of a dog. After that I painted one more, and then one more... Then I felt that painting pets is exactly the thing that inspires me and I really enjoy doing it! When I look at them, I feel that they are trying to tell me something. With each portrait I feel compelled to paint more and to embody new ideas.

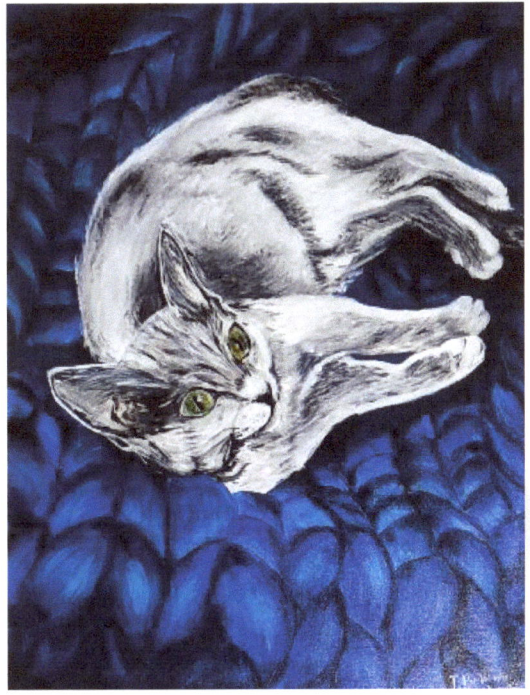
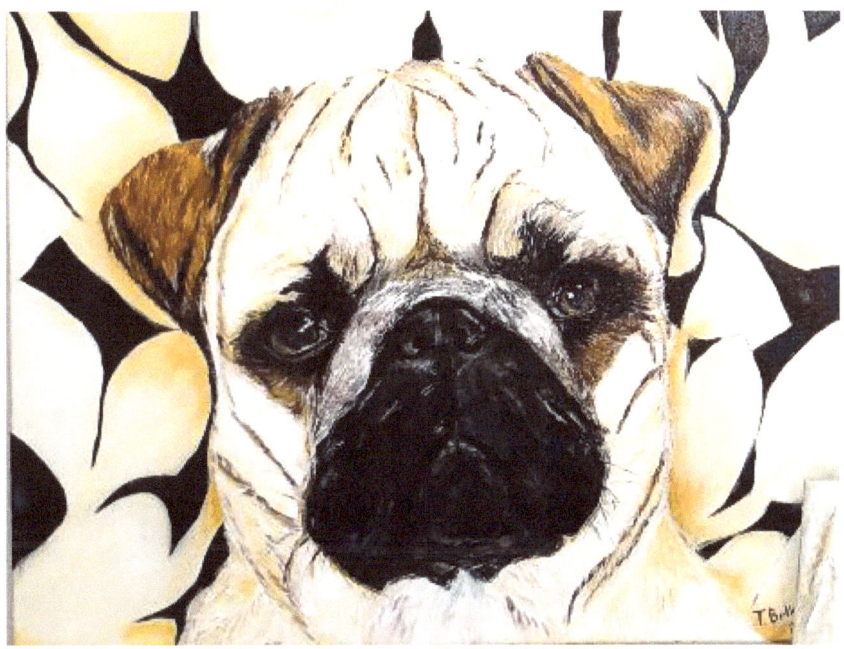
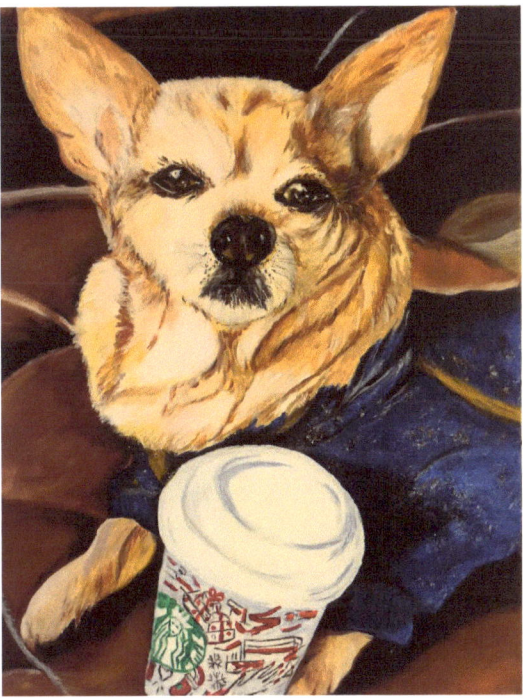
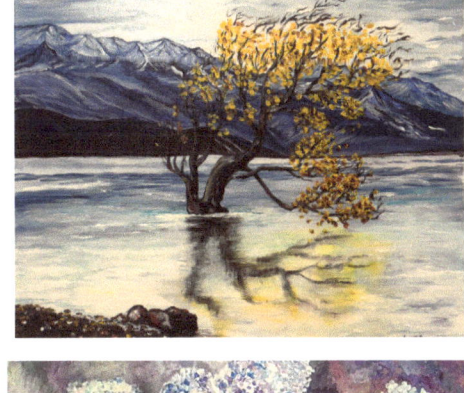
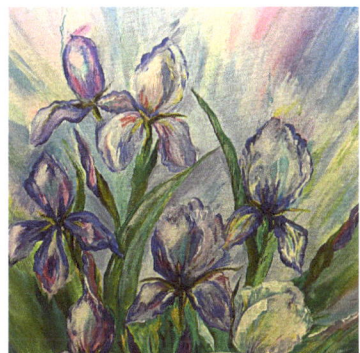
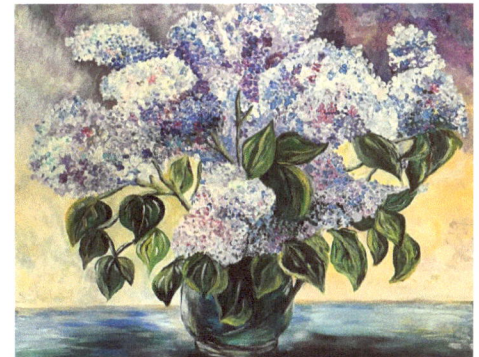
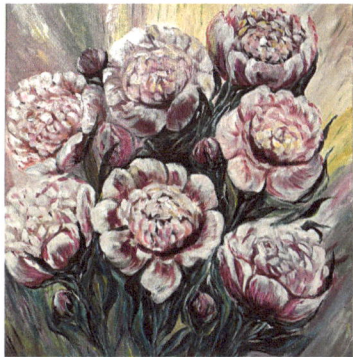

WWW.GARDEAVANT.ORG

APRIL 6 - 8, 2018

INTERNATIONAL SALON OF CONTEMPORARY ART

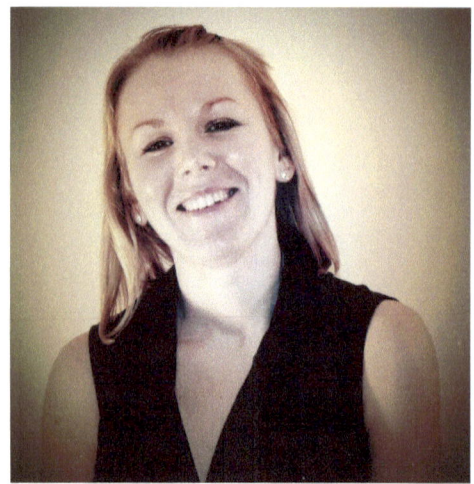

Tatsiana Yukhno

I'm an artist, designer and teacher of art from Belarus. I have a 9 years of professional art education, big experiences of exhibitions in Belarus, Russia and Europe. And I have Grant " Teacher of the Year " on Belarus and any more diplomas and certificates of art.

My fb: www.facebook.com/tatsianayukhno/ArtT"

My Instagram: www.instagram.com/art_by_tatsiana

Zet171819@gmail.com

215-602-6132

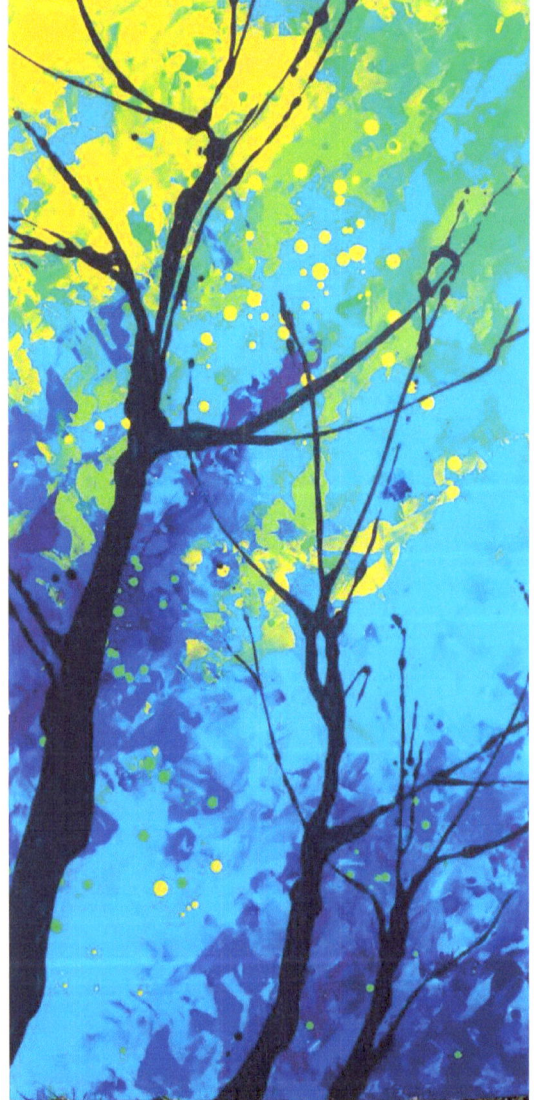
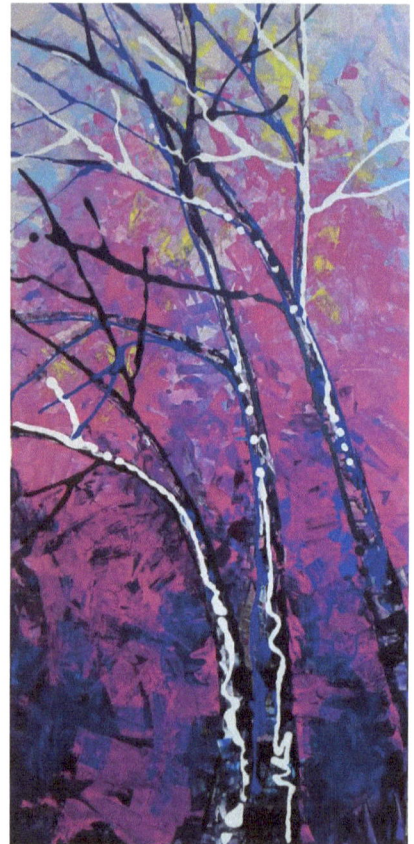
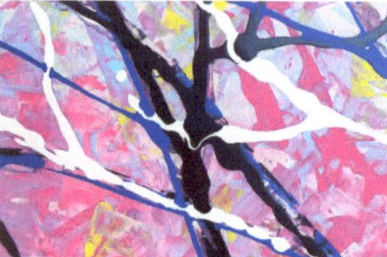
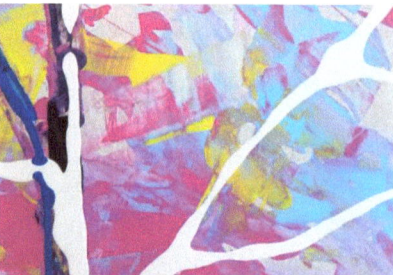
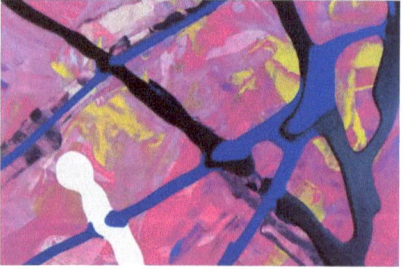
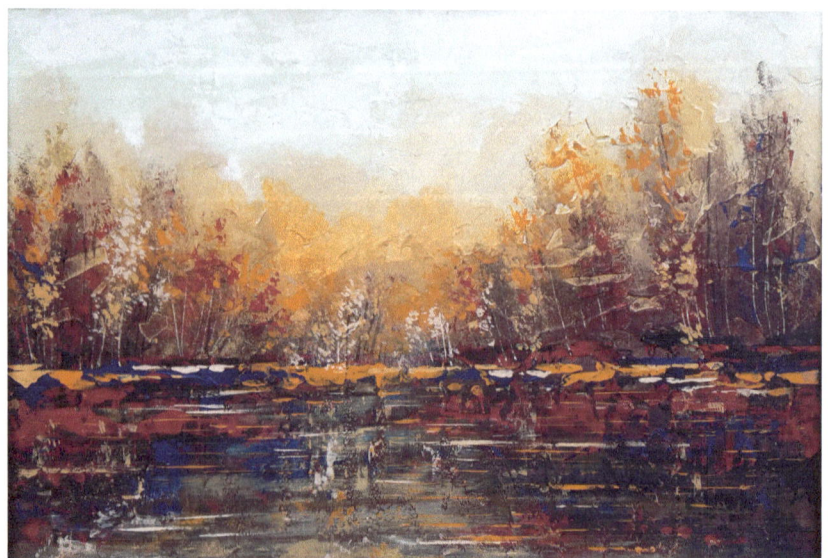

WWW.GARDEAVANT.ORG

APRIL 6 - 8, 2018

International Salon of Contemporary Art

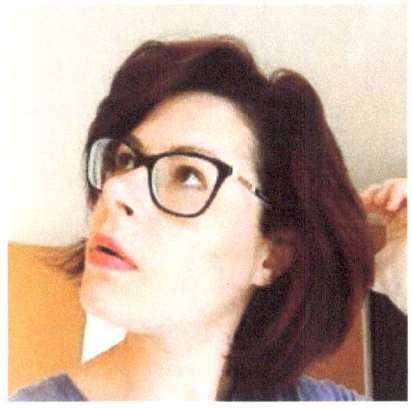

Alla Reznik

- Member of Main Line Art Center
- Member of Wayne Art Center
- Member of DaVinci Art Alliance
- Member of Professional Artist Program at Main Line Art Center

Mobile: **(267) 844 1535**

Email: **allareznikart@gmail.com**

Website: **www.allareznikart.com**

Russian born, my family immigrated to Israel when I was 17. Ten years later I started my own family in the United States. My personality and so is my art are influenced by very different cultures.

I paint subjects which caught my eye during my travels. There is some artwork with a focus on capturing motion, whether it was a running horse or a dancing girl, I was able to find unique ways to express the feeling of movement and put it on a canvas.

Throughout my artistic years I used pencil, charcoal, ink and acrylic, but now I'm all focused on oil. Every painting is started with brushes and finished with strong and bold strokes of a pallet knife, which brings volume to my artwork.

Inspired by impressionism and post impressionism I was able to create my own understanding of color and shape. I can easily ignore true color of landscape, for example, and mix imaginary colors, which will result in a fauvist unrealistic painting. My work is not about realistic colors, it's about how they all work together. I concentrate on values, but not objects, I see and paint dark and light, warm and cool spots.

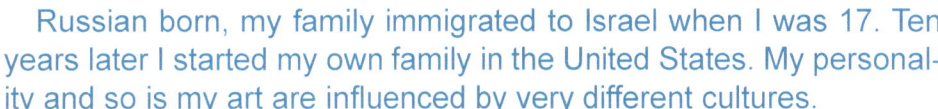
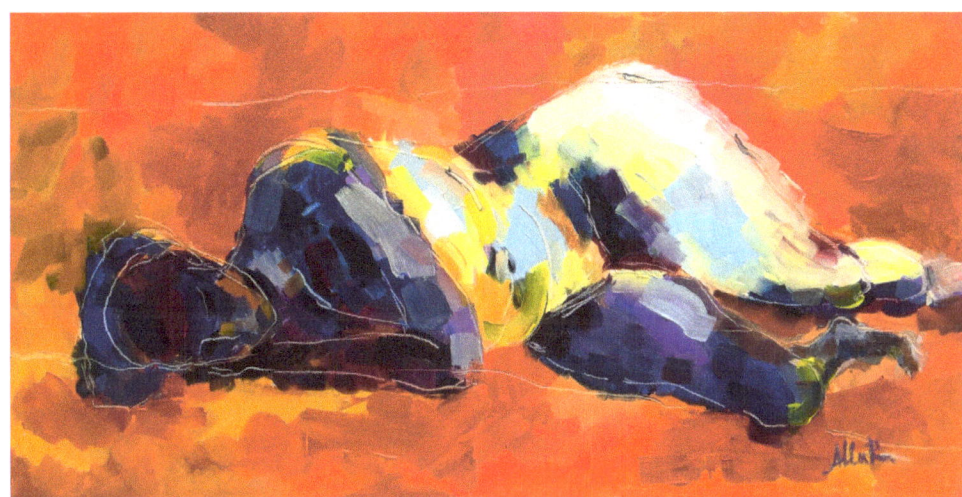
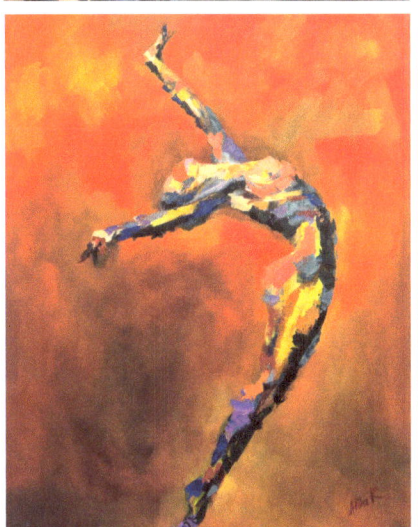
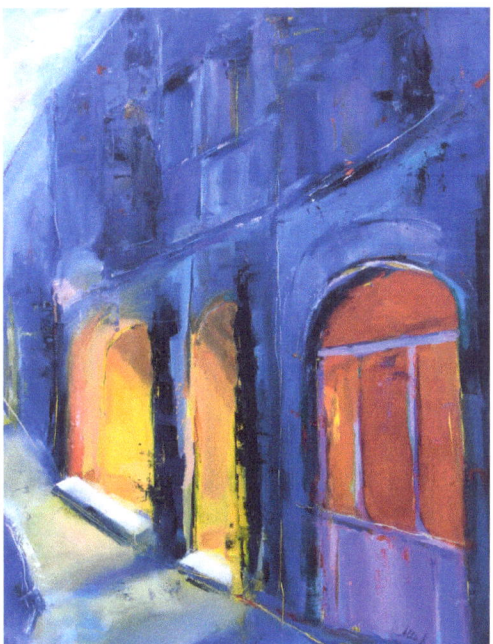
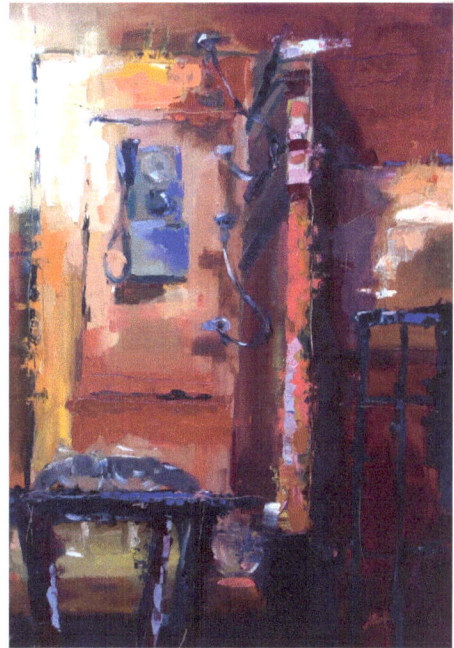

INTERNATIONAL SALON OF CONTEMPORARY ART

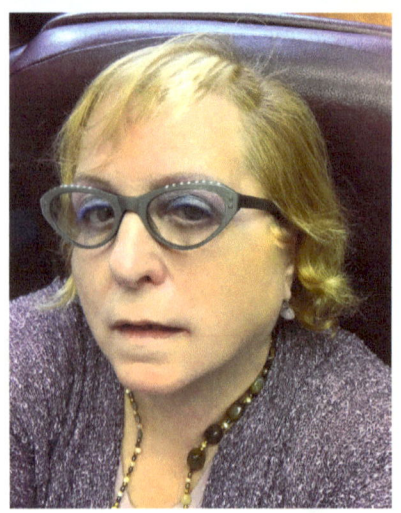

Eleonora Antsis

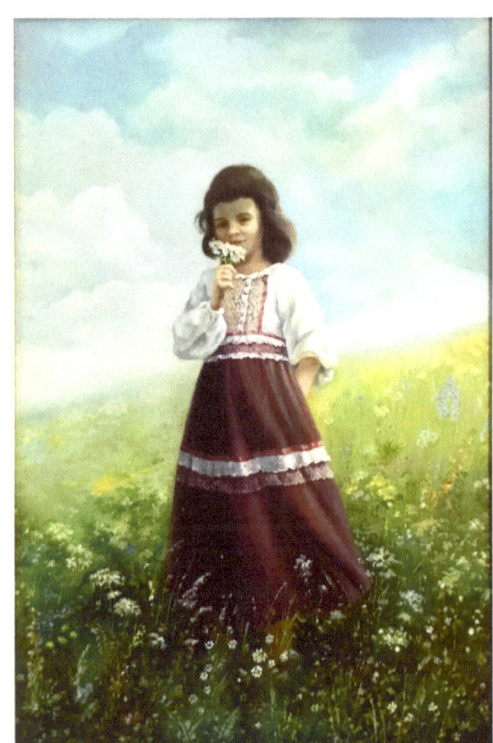

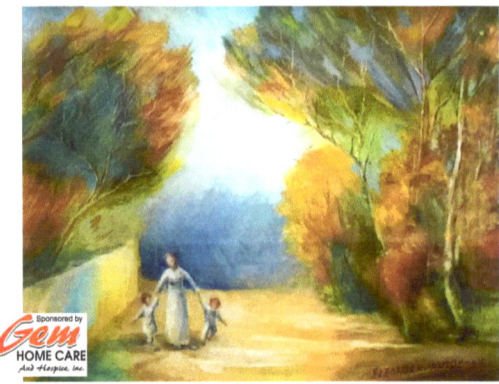

My name is Eleonora Antsis. I immigrated to America from Ukraine in late 1979, and I would like to think about myself as a New Yorker, since I spent the brightest seven years of my American life in New York. I studied Art, Design, Programming, Computer Graphics and Animation at Parsons school of Design and New York University as well as Filmmaking at Global Village.

In 1983, while studying at Parsons, I received a scholarship in Photography from Ansel Adams and was blessed with an opportunity to study photography with the Greatest One at Carmel, California. After moving to Philadelphia I taught Computer Graphics and Programming for Graphics and Animation at Delaware and Bucks County Community Colleges and Moore College of Art.

As an artist, I have been always attracted to themes that allow me to explore "sacred" in my paintings and to unveil the mysterious side of the subjects in my photography. Being deeply influenced by the nobility and austerity of the esthetics of Ansel Adams and Wynn Bullock and Pictorialist style of Josef Sudek, I mostly favor Black and White photography, but I do work in color as well.

In the past few years I became very much passionate about portrait photography (my biggest influence being Arnold Newman and Edward Weston). My involvement with the portrait photography has been given to me an opportunity to connect the sacred and the mundane; to penetrate and reveal the complexity of the human psyche in our life pilgrimage for love and understanding in search for the spirit of our own soul.

I consider the goal of my Art: to visually reflect this existential search, which I see through my inner sight.

I dedicated my artistic imagery to my three children: Antoine, Olivia and Rebecca.

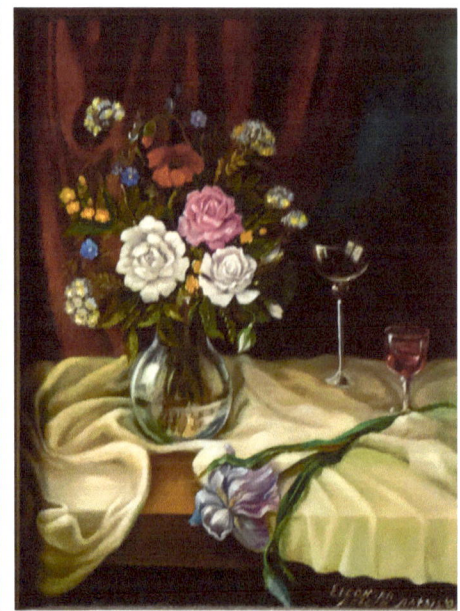

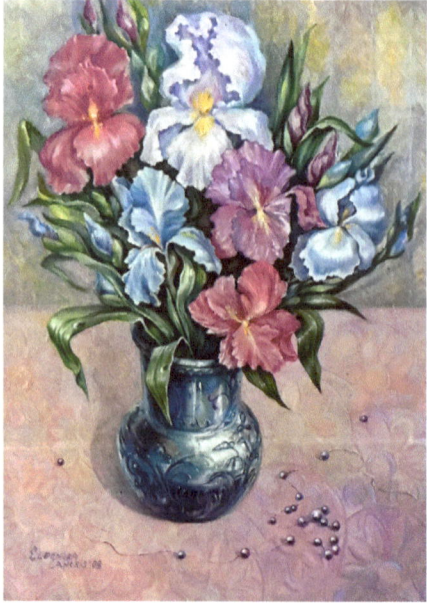

WWW.GARDEAVANT.ORG

APRIL 6 - 8, 2018

INTERNATIONAL SALON OF CONTEMPORARY ART

Eleonora Antsis

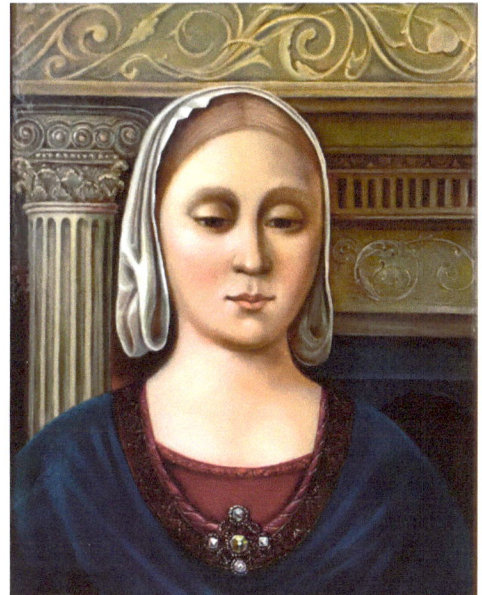
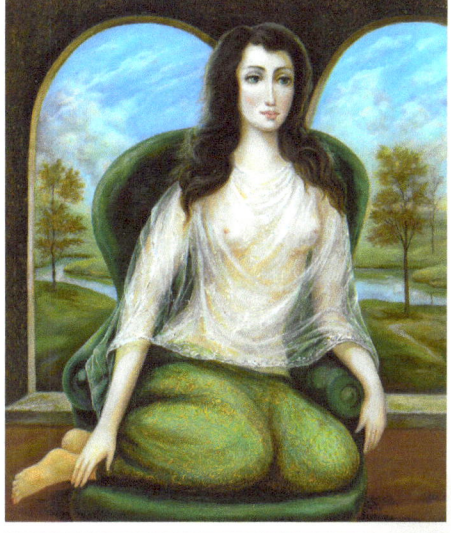
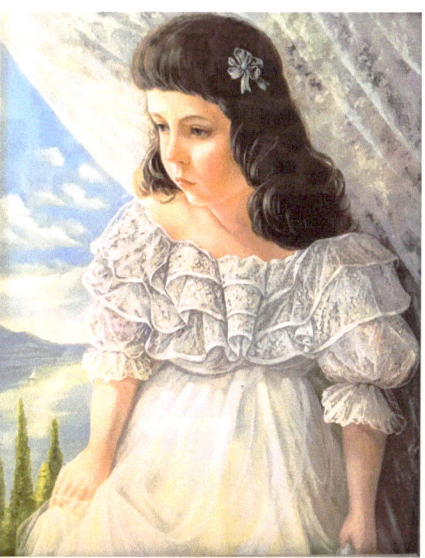
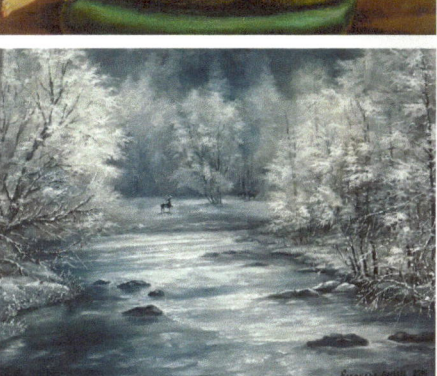
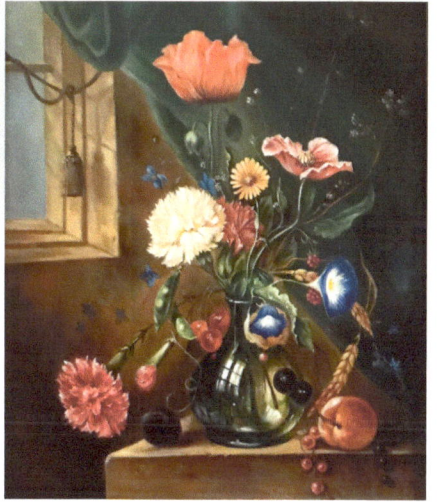
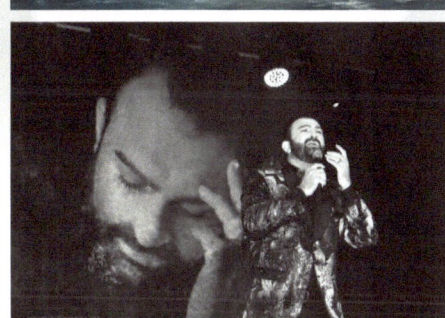
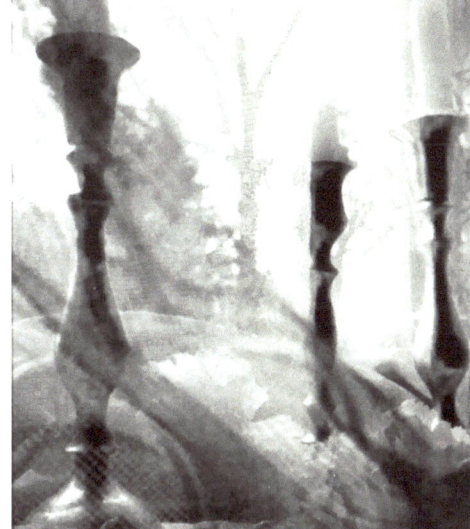
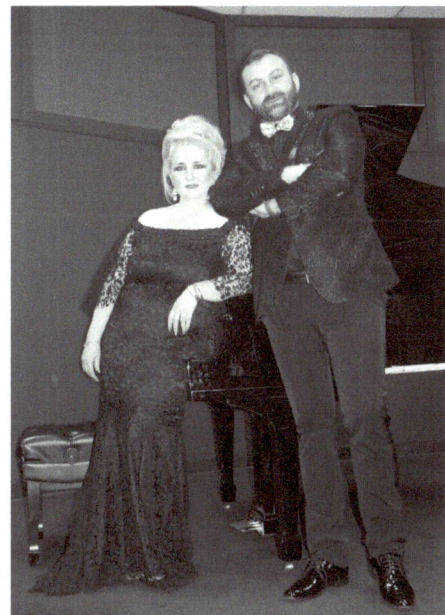
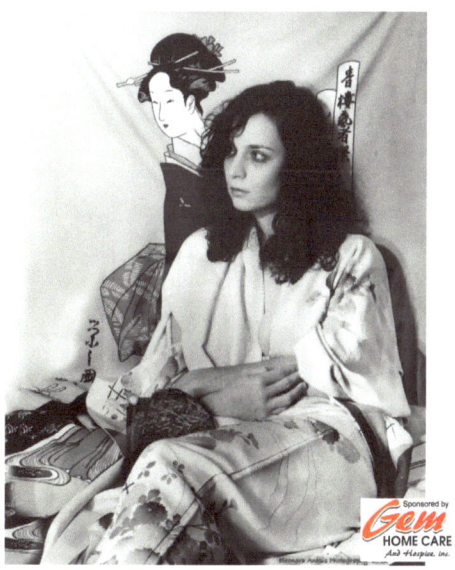

WWW.GARDEAVANT.ORG   APRIL 6 - 8, 2018

International Salon of Contemporary Art

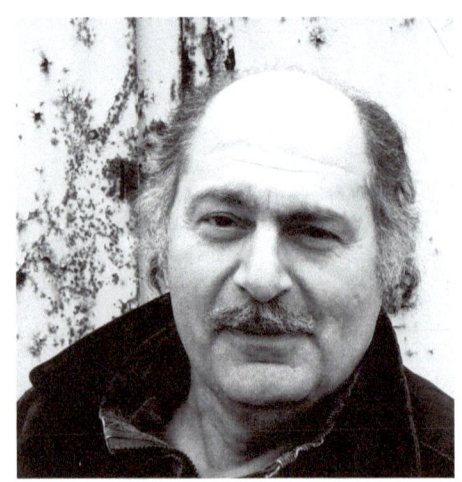

Altai Sadiqzadeh

Born in Baku, Azerbaijan 1951. Lives and works in Baku Altai Sadiqzadeh studied at the Azimzadeh State Art College in Baku. He continued his education at the Faculty of Painting at the Surikov State Academic Art Institute in Moscow in 1971–77. The scope of Sadiqzadeh's artistic practice includes pictorial and graphic work, sculpture and installation, and his work has been featured in many exhibitions since the 1970s. He has been a member of the Union of Artists of the USSR since 1979 and a member of Baku Arts Centre since 1988. His works are held in national and private collections in Azerbaijan, Belgium, France, Germany, Iran, Israel, Norway, Russia, Spain, Switzerland, Turkey, the United Kingdom and the USA.

Altai Sadiqzadeh is the author of the project, the architect, the designer, and the author of the collection and the exhibition of the Museum of Modern Art in Baku.

The interior space, with its sloping walls and without doors or corners, was designed especially with avant-garde art in mind, allowing the art and the building containing it to enjoy a symbiosis. His sculptural metal constructions, installations and painted canvases

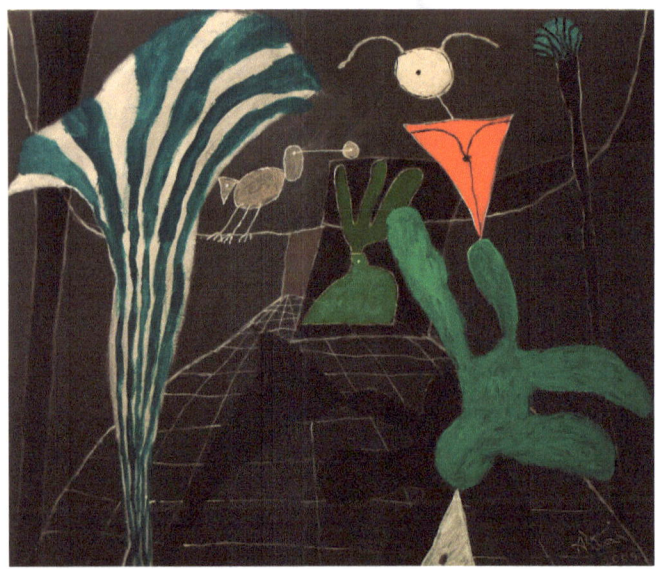
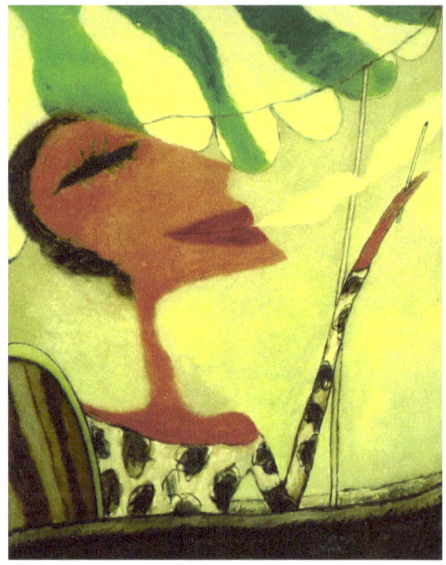
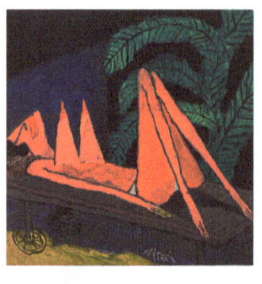
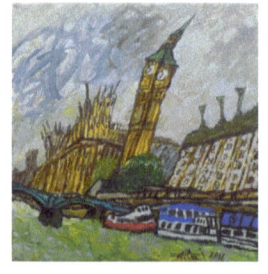
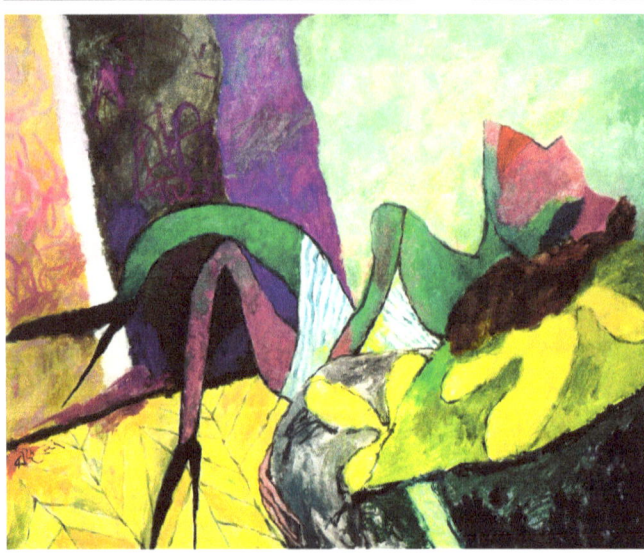
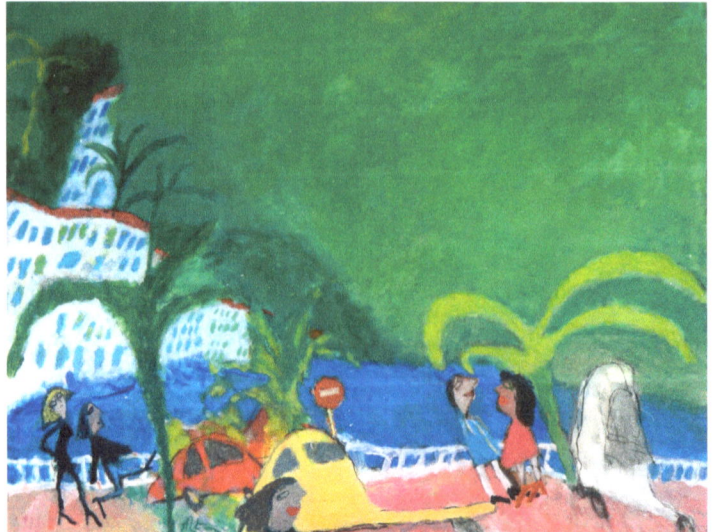

WWW.GARDEAVANT.ORG APRIL 6 - 8, 2018

INTERNATIONAL SALON OF CONTEMPORARY ART

Altai Sadiqzadeh

are incorporated into the museum. He has also been instrumental in selecting the museum's collection and curating its exhibitions.

Sadiqzadeh is primarily known as a painter, who also engages in graphic work and stage design. In recent years, his flexible and visual imagination has led him to explore his ideas in monumental three-dimensional art objects – the series of welded metal constructions entitled The Mechanics of Space. This artist creates his sculptures as if they were multi-dimensional paintings. His work exemplifies a new discovery of the world through its colourful, self-constructing text, teeming with 'apparatuses', hieroglyphs, esoteric epistles, palm trees, anthropomorphic machines, extra-terrestrial 'guardians', star observers and people.

At the 54th Venice Biennale in 2011, Sadiqzadeh exhibited his monumental 'cosmic' canvases and sculptures at the Azerbaijan Pavilion. Looking at them, one sees humanity through the eyes of other worlds and it becomes evident that the possibilities of individual freedom and creative art forms are endless and cannot be limited by anything.

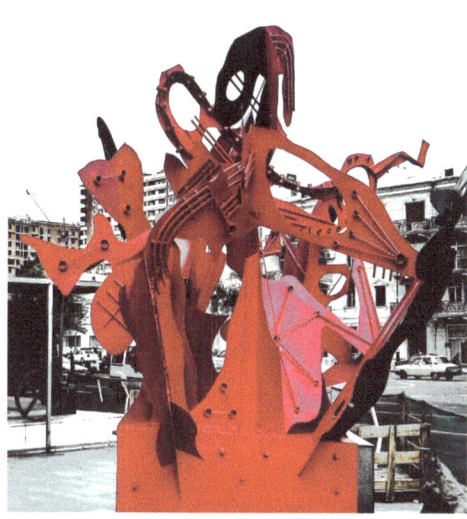

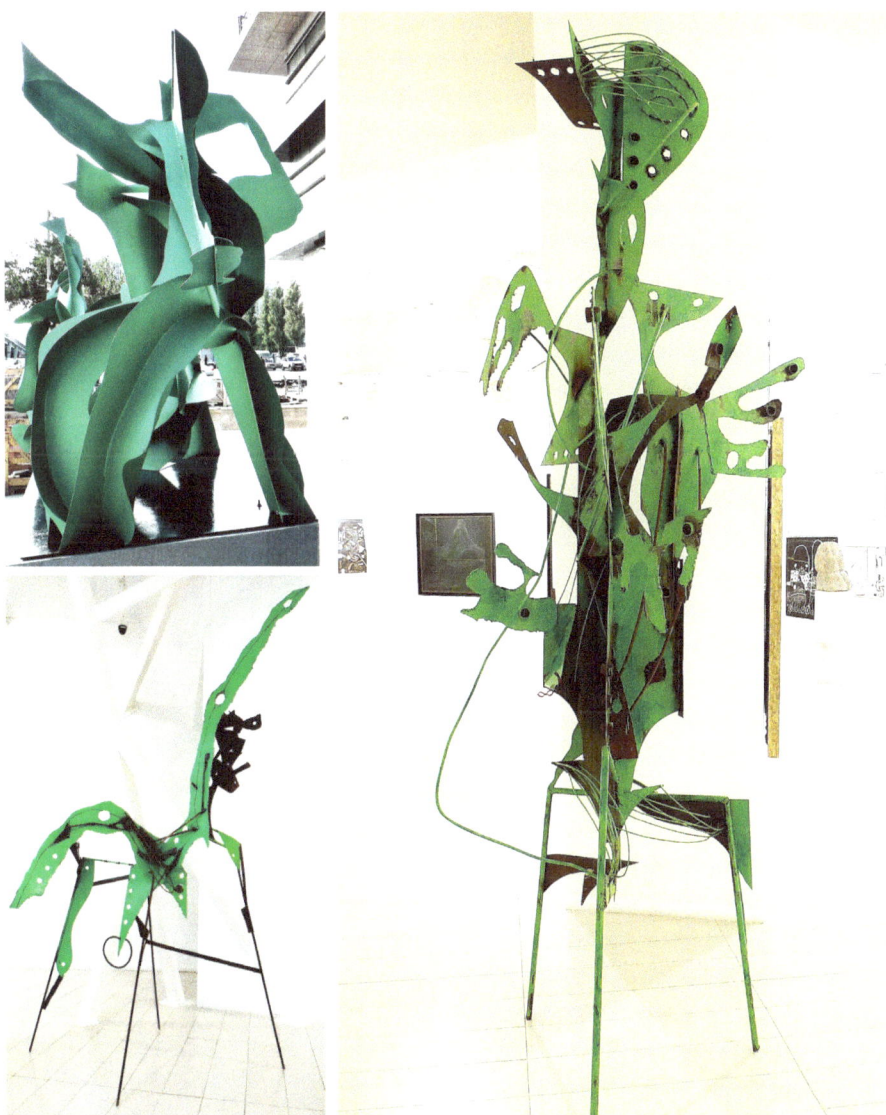

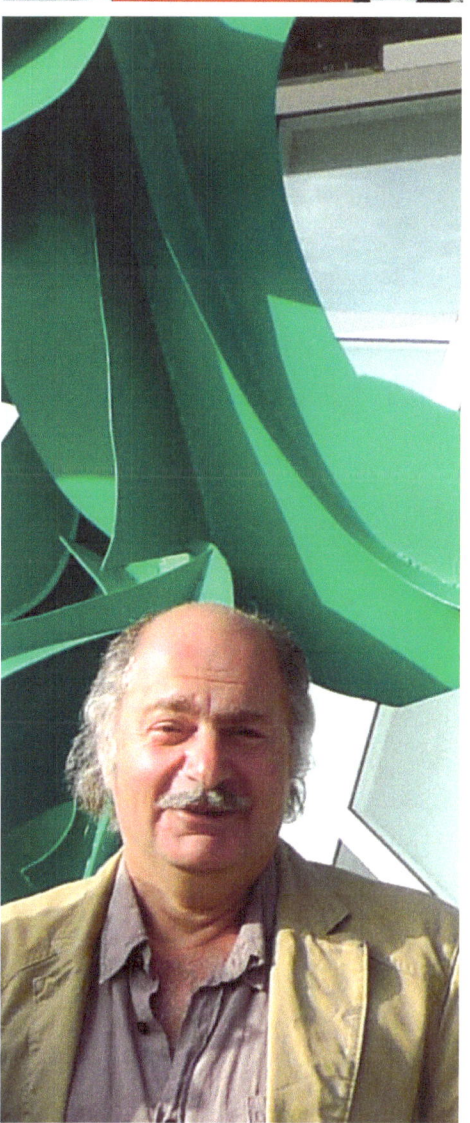

WWW.GARDEAVANT.ORG

APRIL 6 - 8, 2018

INTERNATIONAL SALON OF CONTEMPORARY ART

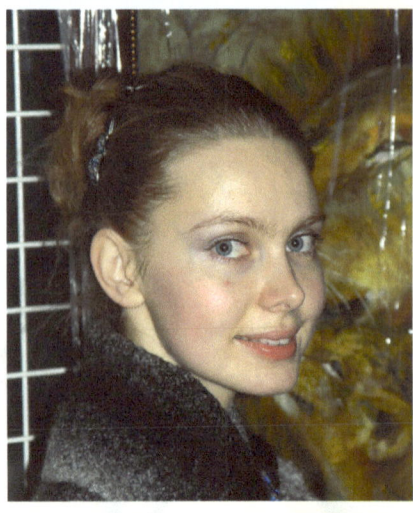

Agnessa Lokshina

Agnes Lokshina was born grew up in Gothic Riga. However, the city in which she became an artist was the modern Kiev. Her artistic credo: ...to create in love, for the God's glory and people's happiness", which Agnes expresses in various techniques - easel painting, graphics, sculpture and ceramics.

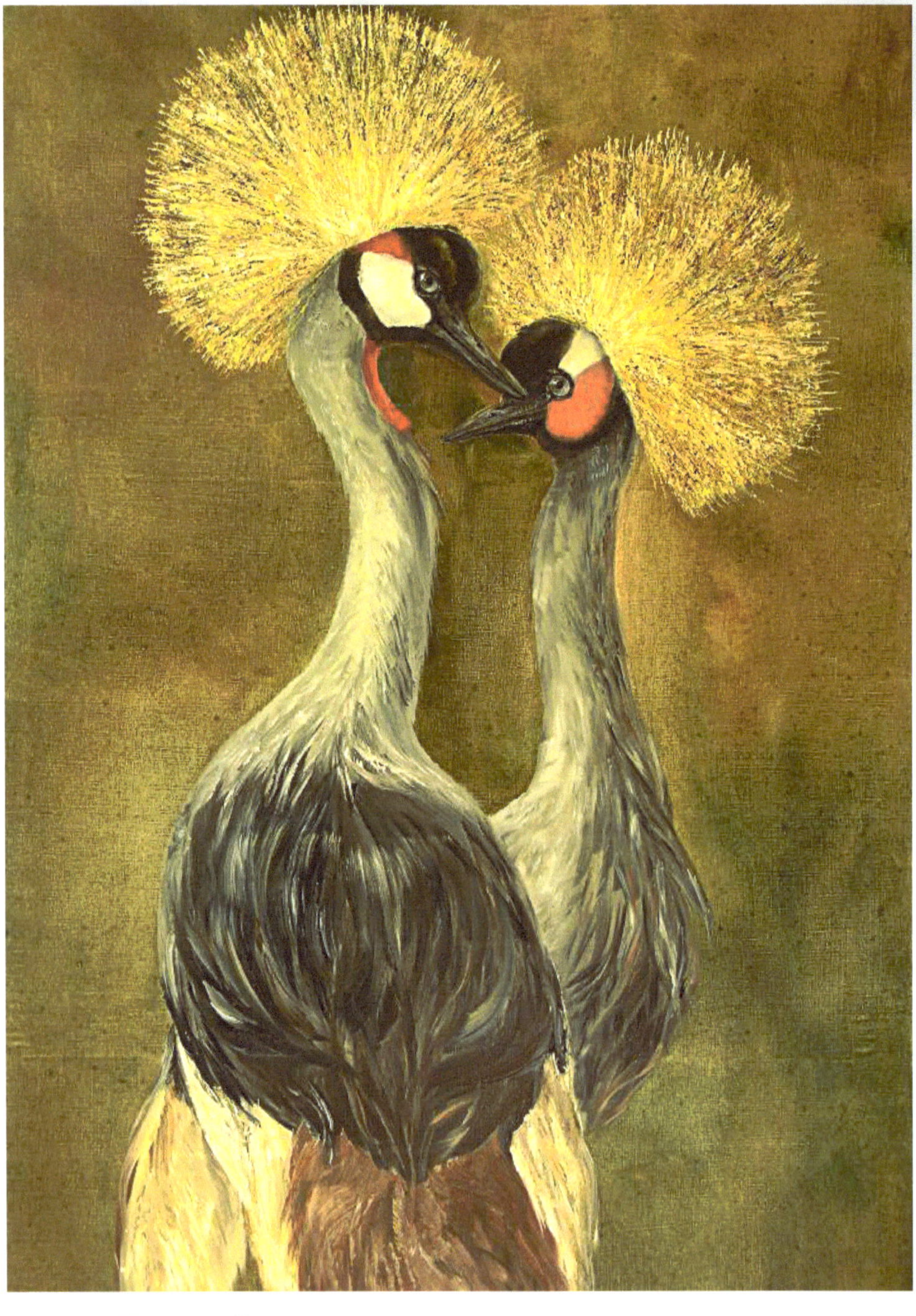

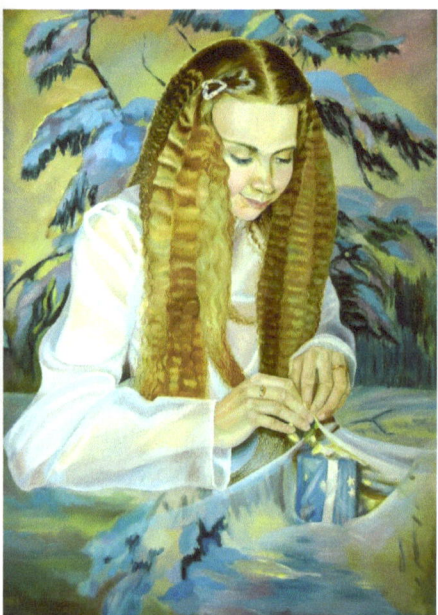

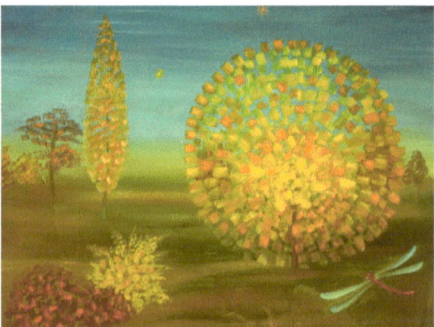

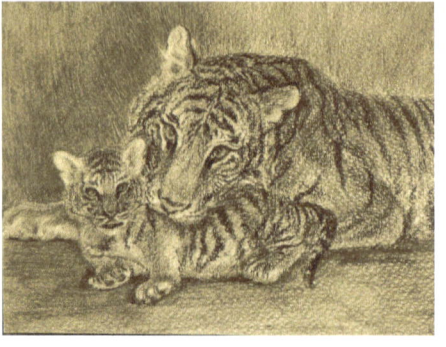

WWW.GARDEAVANT.ORG   APRIL 6 - 8, 2018

International Salon of Contemporary Art

Jeanne Sugira

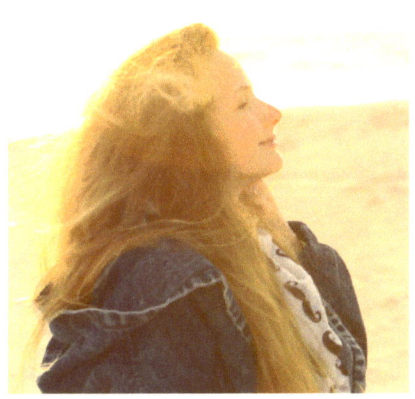

I'm artist from Ashdod, Israel. I create my works in different techniques and genres. I pull my inspiration from traveling in good company, communication, watching literature, music and life. For the exhibition I provide caricatures and illustrations - my travel notes.

Email: *jeannesugira@gmail.com*
Instagrm: *jeannesugira*

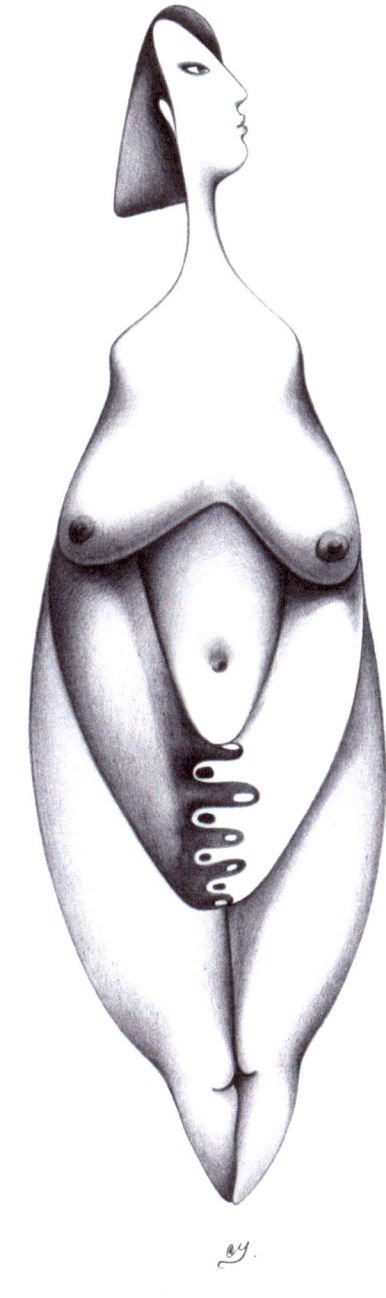

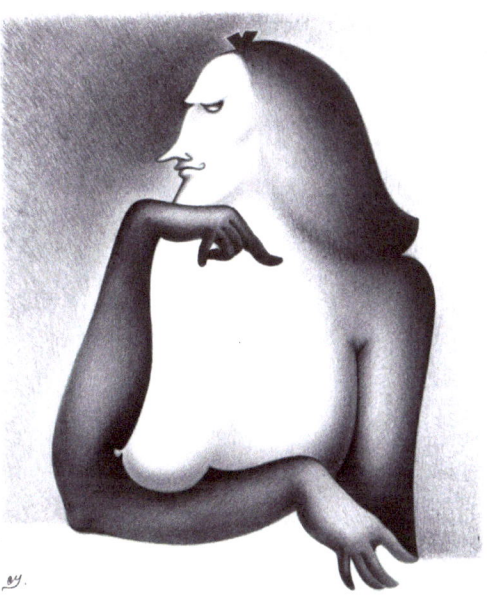

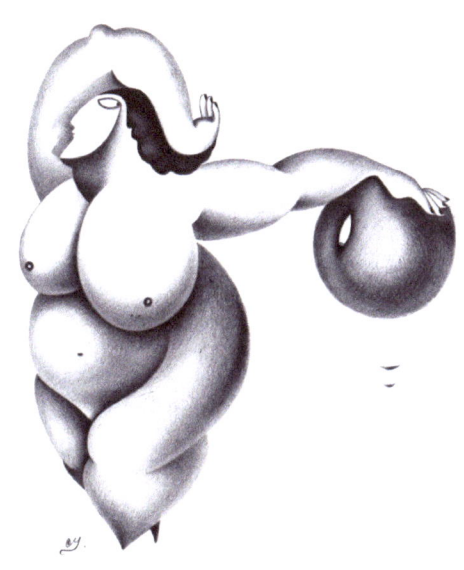

WWW.GARDEAVANT.ORG

APRIL 6 - 8, 2018

INTERNATIONAL SALON OF CONTEMPORARY ART

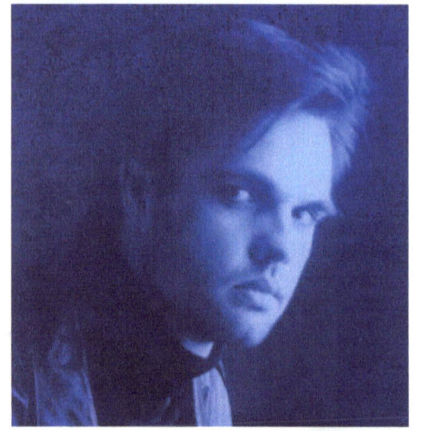

Christopher Jodlowski

As a child I was always drawing and had a love and appreciation for art. However, I did not start painting until July of 2015. I took lessons almost every Saturday for a year from the master artist Paul Gorka. Mr. Gorka saw talent in me and encouraged me to never stop painting.

In September of 2017 I entered four of my paintings in the Adam Styka Art Exhibition at the Shrine of Our Lady of Czestochowa in Doylestown, PA where 32 artists had also entered their works, and I won the "Peoples' Choice Award" for my painting entitled "The Galloping Pair."

I am very grateful to God for the talents that He has given me, and I wish to serve Him well with them.

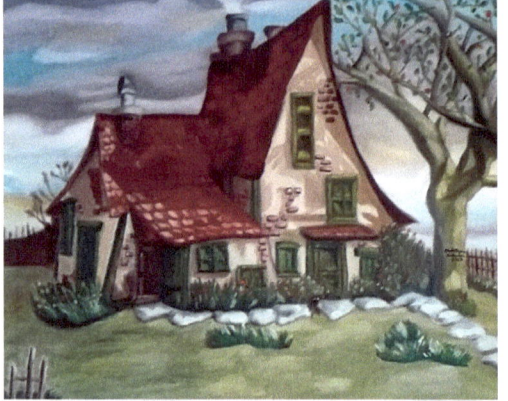
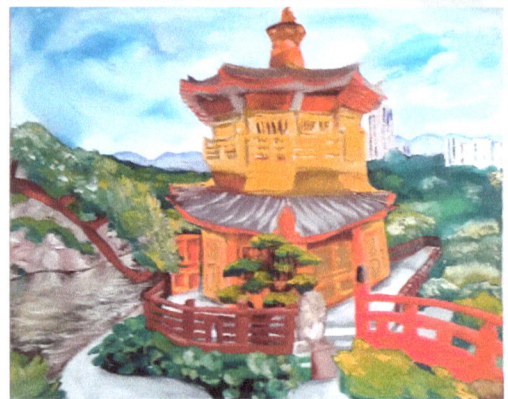
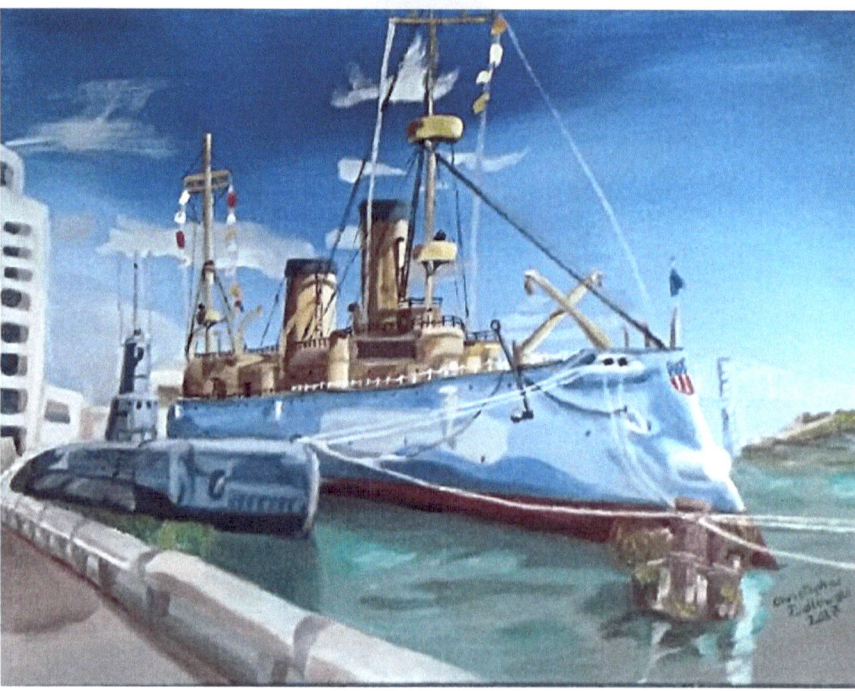
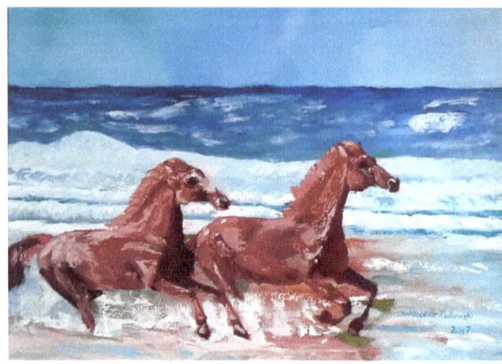
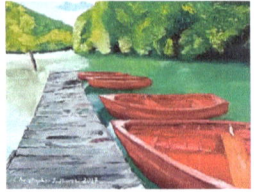
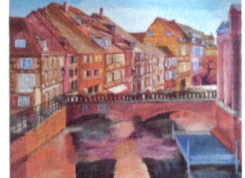
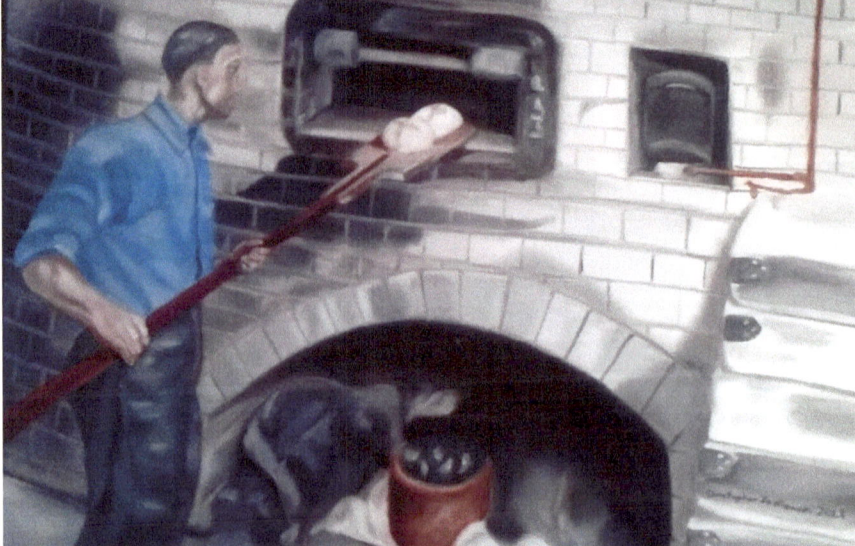

WWW.GARDEAVANT.ORG

APRIL 6 - 8, 2018

INTERNATIONAL SALON OF CONTEMPORARY ART

ARTIST LIST

- **Gennadiy Kaplan,** Pennsylvania, USA
- **Vitaly Rakhman,** Pennsylvania, USA
- **Luda Makarova-Popovich,** Pennsylvania, USA
- **Elena Dobrovolskaya,** New York, USA
- **Leo Hanian,** Pennsylvania, USA
- **Aleksandr E. Kushner,** Colorado, USA
- **Isaak Fishkis,** Pennsylvania, USA
- **Lev Brodsky,** Pennsylvania, USA
- **Kora Velikhanly,** New York, USA
- **Vladislav Rudkin,** New York, USA
- **Lana Vain,** New York, USA
- **Emanue Antsis,** Pennsylvania, USA
- **Diana Korobov,** Pennsylvania, USA
- **Sarra Rudkin-Peysakh,** Pennsylvania, USA
- **Tetiana Belkina,** Pennsylvania, USA
- **Tatsiana Yukhno,** Pennsylvania, USA
- **Alla Reznik,** Pennsylvania, USA
- **Eleonora Antsis,** Pennsylvania, USA
- **Altai Sadiqzadeh,** Azerbaijan
- **Agnessa Lokshina,** Urkaina
- **Jeanne Sugira,** Israel
- **Christopher Jodlowski,** Pennsylvania, USA

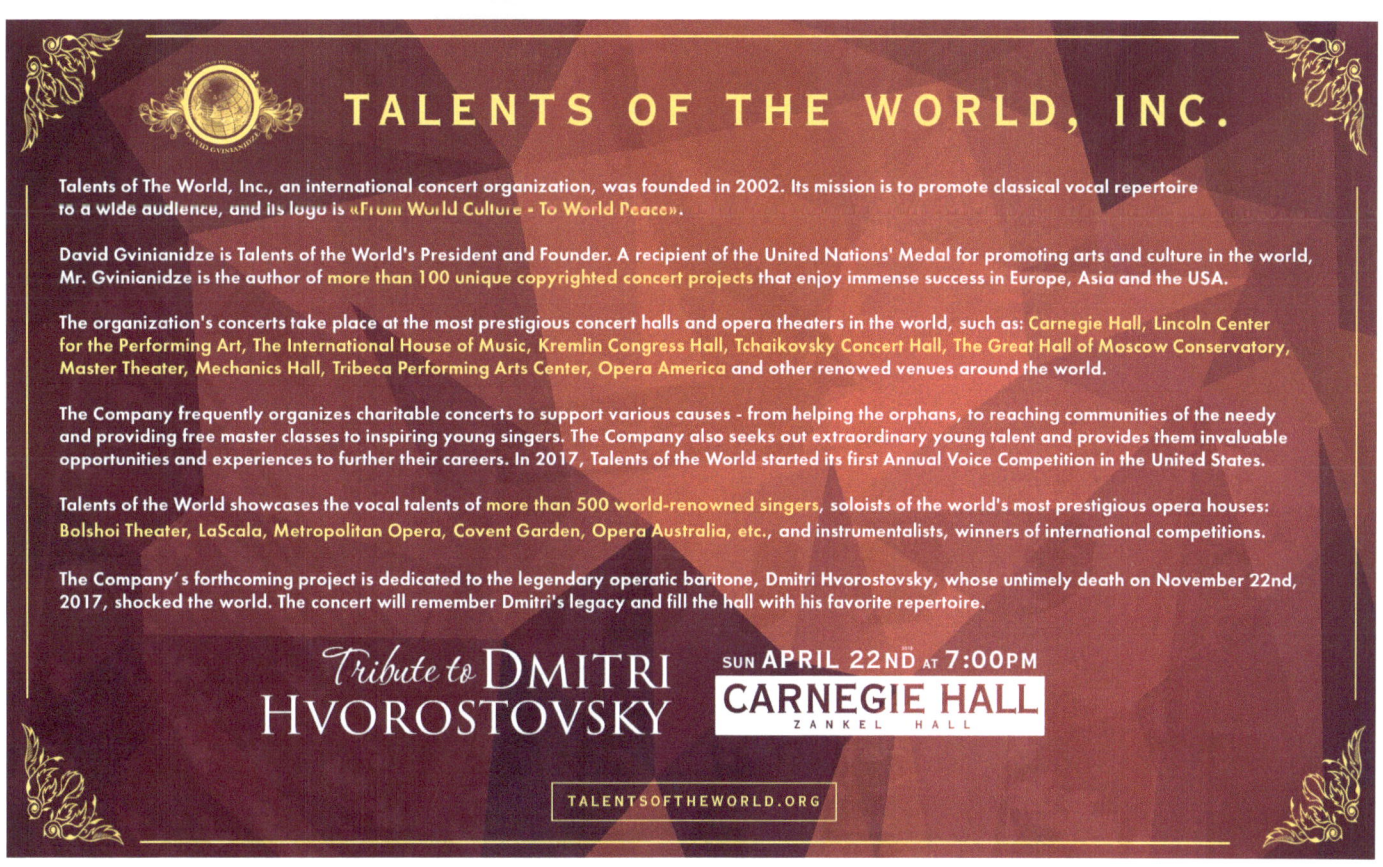

TALENTS OF THE WORLD, INC.

Talents of The World, Inc., an international concert organization, was founded in 2002. Its mission is to promote classical vocal repertoire to a wide audience, and its logo is «From World Culture - To World Peace».

David Gvinianidze is Talents of the World's President and Founder. A recipient of the United Nations' Medal for promoting arts and culture in the world, Mr. Gvinianidze is the author of more than 100 unique copyrighted concert projects that enjoy immense success in Europe, Asia and the USA.

The organization's concerts take place at the most prestigious concert halls and opera theaters in the world, such as: Carnegie Hall, Lincoln Center for the Performing Art, The International House of Music, Kremlin Congress Hall, Tchaikovsky Concert Hall, The Great Hall of Moscow Conservatory, Master Theater, Mechanics Hall, Tribeca Performing Arts Center, Opera America and other renowed venues around the world.

The Company frequently organizes charitable concerts to support various causes - from helping the orphans, to reaching communities of the needy and providing free master classes to inspiring young singers. The Company also seeks out extraordinary young talent and provides them invaluable opportunities and experiences to further their careers. In 2017, Talents of the World started its first Annual Voice Competition in the United States.

Talents of the World showcases the vocal talents of more than 500 world-renowned singers, soloists of the world's most prestigious opera houses: Bolshoi Theater, LaScala, Metropolitan Opera, Covent Garden, Opera Australia, etc., and instrumentalists, winners of international competitions.

The Company's forthcoming project is dedicated to the legendary operatic baritone, Dmitri Hvorostovsky, whose untimely death on November 22nd, 2017, shocked the world. The concert will remember Dmitri's legacy and fill the hall with his favorite repertoire.

Tribute to **DMITRI HVOROSTOVSKY**

SUN APRIL 22ND AT 7:00PM
CARNEGIE HALL ZANKEL HALL

TALENTSOFTHEWORLD.ORG

INTERNATIONAL SALON OF CONTEMPORARY ART

SPONSORS

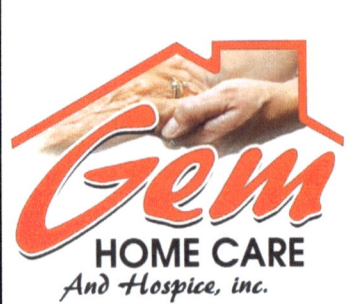

Quality Home Health Servives

55 Buck Road, Suite 9
Huntingdon Valley, PA 19006

215.396.4950

www.gemhomecare.com

Being there is why I'm here.

Total average savings of **$894***
when you combine home and auto.
Call my office for a quote 24/7.

Marat Ioshpa, Agent
8420 Bustleton Avenue
Philadelphia, PA 19152
Bus: 215-305-5555
marat.ioshpa.rnko@statefarm

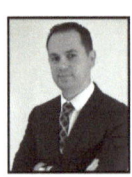

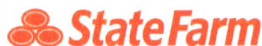 **State Farm**

*Average annual per household savings based on a 2016 national survey of new policyholders who reported savings by switching to State Farm.
State Farm Mutual Automobile Insurance Company, State Farm Indemnity Company, State Farm Fire and Casualty Company, State Farm General Insurance Company, Bloomington, IL
P097186.1

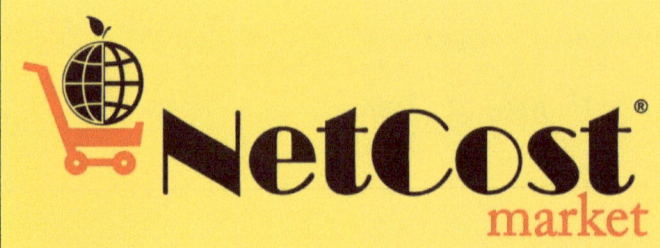

Insurance To Protect the items you love anywhere in the World.

We Insure: Fine Art, Collectibles, Musical Instruments, Jewelry, Furs, Cameras and much more.

Marat Ioshpa Agent
Bus: 215 305 5555
Fax: 215 613 5361

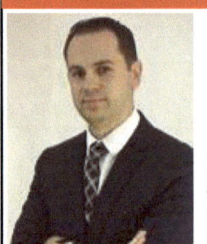

ЕВРЕЙСКАЯ ЖИЗНЬ
JEWISH LIFE
חיים יהודים

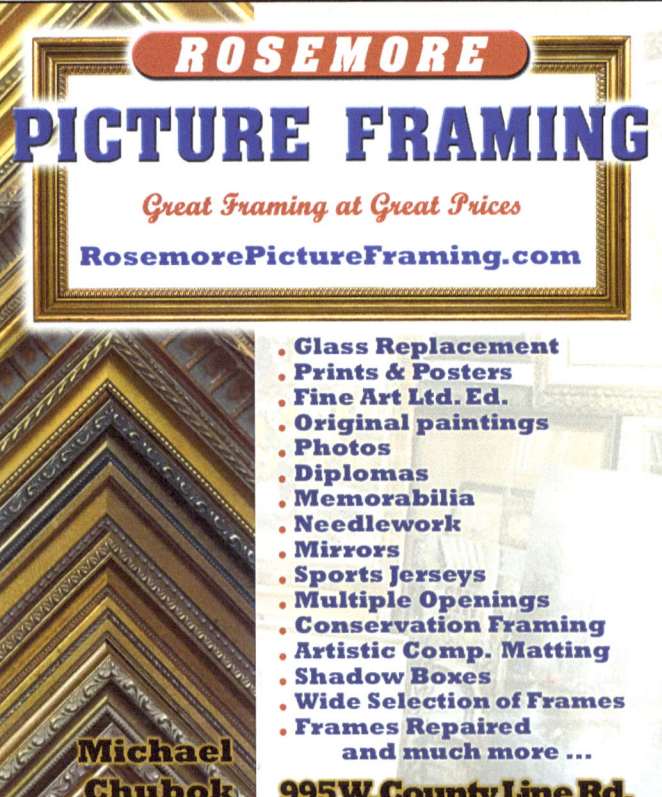

РЕКЛАМА жизнь
www.adandlife.com

PILGRIM TRAVEL GROUP
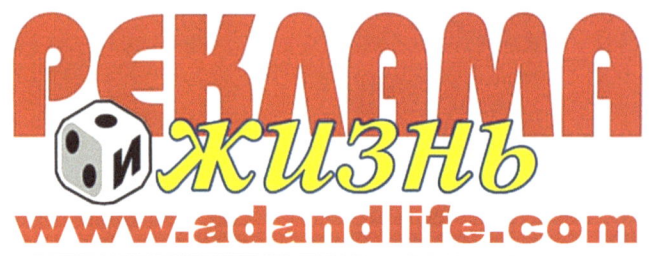
www.pilgrim-group.org
1-877-707-8787

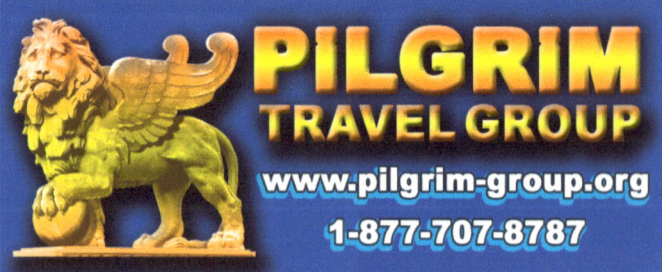

A Print Zone
aprintzone@aol.com
Tel: **267.304.1823**

Corporate Identity ↔ Logos ↔ Business Cards
Brochures ↔ Fliers ↔ Postcards ↔ Magnets
Booklets ↔ Catalogues ↔ Books

WWW.GARDEAVANT.ORG   APRIL 6 - 8, 2018

www.ingramcontent.com/pod-product-compliance
Lightning Source LLC
Chambersburg PA
CBHW041936240526
45473CB00034B/1721